W9-DHG-232

Welcome

to MMA's Living Stewardship Series!

As a church-related organization dedicated to helping people live lives of
Christian stewardship, MMA is pleased to provide this resource as part of
the *Living Stewardship Series.*

MMA exists to help Christians answer God's call to care for and cultivate
the gifts God has given them. To accomplish this, we offer products,
services, and resources – like this study book. Our goal is to help you
understand biblical principles of stewardship while, at the same time,
providing real world ways you can incorporate those principles into your
everyday living.

The Bible tells us we are to seek wholeness in our lives. In the Gospel
of Matthew (5:48) Jesus said in his Sermon on the Mount to *"Be perfect,
therefore, as your heavenly Father is perfect."* But, who among us can
ever be perfect?

Actually, the Greek word traditionally translated as "perfect" in that verse
is *teleios* – which means, "to be whole." *Living Stewardship* is not a series
for perfect people, but for people like you who are seeking wholeness.
People who don't want to leave their faith in Christ at the church door after
Sunday worship. People who want that faith to color how they relate to
family and friends, how they work at their jobs, how they spend their
money, how they take care of themselves – essentially, how they live.

At MMA, "holistic" refers to the essential interconnectedness of all the elements of Christian stewardship. For the sake of simplicity, we've identified the crucial elements as time, relationships, finances, health, and talents. Integrating all five, and nurturing the relationships between them, produces a healthy life of holistic stewardship. MMA feels strongly about holistic stewardship – so strongly, in fact, that we have reoriented our approach to stewardship to recognize this interconnectedness of all parts of our lives.

On the stewardship path of your life, you will find the journey easier if you pay attention to all of these areas of your life and recognize how they work together to lead you to the wholeness of God. If one of these elements becomes unbalanced, broken, or disconnected, you experience a lack of wholeness. However, with a strong core (faith) connecting each area, and careful attention to each area as needed, God's love can flow through you and produce wholeness in your life – and in the lives of others you touch.

What is MMA?

MMA is a church-related organization that helps Christians practice biblical stewardship.

We are the stewardship agency of Mennonite Church USA, but MMA also serves other faith communities affiliated with the Anabaptist tradition. MMA helps you pursue stewardship solutions through insurance and financial services, charitable giving, and other stewardship resources, as well as with our educational resources, such as this study book, and stewardship education events through Stewardship University.

MMA wants to help you live a holistic life of stewardship centered on Christ – and become the best steward of God's resources you can.

This is why we believe *holistic stewardship* involves much more than just the products and services MMA provides. Holistic stewardship looks at the *interconnectedness* that weaves through the areas of our lives. And, as Christians, it's all filtered through our faith in Christ. This faith is what drives the search for wholeness.

How good a steward you are in your finances, can affect your health and your relationships. If you are having trouble with your health, that can affect how you are able to use your talents or your time each day. If you're overcommitted and your day feels too full, you may opt to give short shrift to your children or your job. And on it goes. There are countless ways our search for wholeness is affected by our shortcomings in these areas.

MMA®

Stewardship Solutions

Practical tips to keep you moving!

This study book is on using your God-given talents – but in this study you won't find tips about vocal technique, acting methods, or how to structure a three-point sermon. What you'll study in these pages is how your talents, and your stewardship of them, affect your lives and the lives of those around you. Each of us has a minimum of one talent given to him or her by God. Most have more than one. Maybe you don't feel you can use these talents for God, or you don't even know what your talents are. But if you're not using your gifts and talents fully, what does that mean if you're a Christian seeking God and wholeness?

Because of the holistic nature of stewardship, don't be surprised when we also talk about your health, time, finances, and relationships – specifically as they relate to your talents

We'll give you practical ways to implement the suggestions we make here – not just open-ended theories! Each chapter ends with discussion questions you can answer as a group, or individually, that will help you identify areas where you may need to do some repair work.

Finally, each book in this series will present you with an implementation plan that will help you identify some key steps you can take *right now*.

There's more!

If you like what you learn here, look for other study guides in the *Living Stewardship Series.*

If you want to learn more about us, visit MMA-online, our home on the Web (www.mma-online.org). There you can find more information and tools to help you on your stewardship journey. You'll also find connections to the MMA partners in your area who can help you achieve the steward-ship goals you have for your life.

Talent Show

Your Faith in Full Color

by Bob Lichty

MMA®

Stewardship Solutions

Goshen, Indiana

Co-published with Herald Press

Talent Show

Living Stewardship Series

Copyright © 2005 by MMA, Goshen, Ind. 46527. All rights reserved.
Co-published with Herald Press, Scottdale, Pa. 15683
Printed in the United States of America

Library of Congress Cataloging-in-Publication Data
Lichty, Bob, 1969-
Talent show: your faith in full color / by Bob Lichty.
p. cm.
ISBN 0-8361-9319-9 (pbk. : alk. paper)
1. Christian life. 2. Gifts, Spiritual. I. Title.
BV4501.3.L54 2005
248.4–dc22

2005017508

Cover design by Tom Duckworth
Edited by Michael Ehret

MMA®

Stewardship Solutions

1110 North Main Street
Post Office Box 483
Goshen, IN 46527

Toll-free: (800) 348-7468
Telephone: (574) 533-9511
www.mma-online.org

Acknowledgements

To God, for my unique mix of gifts, talents, passions, style, and experience, and to Jen, Taylor, Emma, and Grace, my family, for your love and support. Also, thank you to the following people for their support: Steve Ganger, Mom, Pastor Tim Rowland, Scott Allen, Scott Tilley, Phil Kiefer, Palmer Becker, Andrew Kreider, Tom Hilliker, and Michael Ehret.

Contents

First Word: All for Nothing

Every good and perfect gift is a gift from above, coming down from the Father of the heavenly lights, who does not change like shifting shadows. (*James 1:17*)

Do you know people who constantly toil away yet feel no satisfaction? Are you one of them? In this passage, James tells the 12 tribes of Israel that they will continue to toil in frustration unless they realize they are doing it for God. If you feel you're toiling in frustration, perhaps you're toiling for the wrong reasons. Do any of these thoughts apply to you? Do you:

- Feel as if your talents are being wasted? (*I could be doing so much more.*)

- Feel as if you leave your God-given abilities at church on Sunday? (*That is my church life; this is my everyday life.*)

- Work and work for what this world tells you is important, only to end up feeling empty? (*How can I ever find satisfaction?*)

- Wonder what God's plan is for you? (*Why am I even here?*)

You are not alone. Millions of people spend their lives using their abilities to try and reach personal goals they've set based on what the world expects. Instead of enjoying fulfillment, they often find it was all for naught, feeling little sense of accomplishment when they've reached their goals. Is this what God intended? Of course not.

You don't have to live like this. There is a better way.

All for one

I have worked for small secular companies, mid-sized Christian organizations, and multi-billion dollar secular corporations. I have traveled the world and met people of all races, genders, socioeconomic levels, and religious backgrounds. Nearly all of them claim at least one, if not all, of the following statements:

- I wonder if there is any value in what I am doing.

- My everyday life and church life seem at odds.

- I have taken a spiritual gifts test, and I know my talents, but I still feel unfulfilled.

- My relationships, finances, and even health suffer because of endless quests to find the right place to fit.

People are living lives in which they are trying to use the gifts and talents God has given them to achieve the goals of the world. This leaves them feeling empty inside – searching for a purpose. They may work hard in their congregation on Sunday, but the rest of the week they feel completely detached from God.

This is not what God intended. If our "All for One" is "All for Me," we will be forever empty. Even if it seems to the rest of society that we have the perfect job, house, car, spouse, kids, and pets – we may still end up tossing and turning at night because our souls are not fulfilled.

I coach youth sports – and I love it. But I always feel for the kids who play solely because their parents have pushed them to. It's painfully obvious who these kids are. They try and try, but just can't grasp it. And with each strikeout, each goal they let go by, they look to the stands with a sad expression believing (sometimes rightly) that they've disappointed their parents. These kids are struggling against the pressures of the world, instead of finding, honing, and using their God-given abilities.

Don't we often do the same? We push through business decisions that are morally questionable. We leave our musical instruments or artistic canvases in a closet gathering dust because we're too busy chasing worldly pursuits. Then on Sunday, we look sadly toward our Father and wonder if God is disappointed in us or even aware of our struggles.

Unfortunately, this kind of life deeply affects our relationship with God.

Unfortunately, while this kind of life affects us, it also affects those around us and, ultimately, deeply affects our relationship with God. After all, it was God who gave us these gifts and talents. In James' letter, he strongly urges the Israelites to turn away from their sinful ways. Turn away from using their gifts and talents for personal gain. He reminds them that all things come from God and should be used for good.

How about you? Are you finding it too easy to separate your life on Sunday from the rest of the week? Are you struggling because you want to have your gifts and talents reflect God more? Are you growing closer to God or are you growing closer to the world?

Pleasing God – every day

If you're active in your congregation, you may have taken some type of spiritual gifts assessment at some point. Churches use these tools to help members find places to serve within the congregation. And secular bookstores are filled with resources to help you make the most of your talents and abilities to achieve great success.

Ah-ha! Therein lies the contradiction. Spiritual gifts = church life. But, talents and abilities = everyday life. It shouldn't be this way. The Bible offers great guidance and calls us to use our gifts and abilities in the whole of our life – not just on Sunday. The Bible also assures us God does have a plan for us, and that we often have to look beyond our spiritual gifts and talents to see the whole picture.

Sunday and every day

The challenge of knowing what our gifts and talents are – and then using them in our daily life as opposed to just on Sunday – is a difficult one. But the Bible instructs us to live for God every day! This should be enough to cause us to look for ways to use our gifts and talents for God on a daily basis.

The core principle of this study guide is that it is time to use our talents to give All for One – All for God – All the Time.

The contradiction of living one way on Sunday and another way throughout the week was the impetus for this book. The first 10 lessons focus on five views of abilities: spiritual gifts, talents, passions, style, and experience. All five are examined from both a church and everyday perspective. The last two lessons focus on how to take action in both areas of your life to draw them closer together, so you can use your talents and gifts seamlessly – instead of dividing them between two worlds.

The abilities you use in your everyday life should not contradict those you use on Sunday. Your gifts and talents ought to draw you nearer to God – not push God further away. I pray this study will help you do that.

Gifts

Church Life: Your Spiritual Gifts are for the Church

God has also given each of us different gifts to use. *(Romans 12:6)*

Forest – meet the trees

Tell me if you know this person. George makes a commitment to become more dedicated to, or involved in, the church. So he pours his all into a ministry – teaching, nursery, choir, usher – you name it, George goes for it. Too often, people like George – with their heart in all the right places – simply flame out. They float from one ministry to the other, abandoning each with reasons such as, "It didn't feel right," or "It wasn't what I thought it would be," or "It just wasn't what I wanted to do."

I know George. I know several Georges. In fact, I have been George. Filled with excitement and exuberance for the Lord and my church, I pursued each opportunity with relentless ambition. While I've continued a few of those early ministries – even through the process of relocating and attending a different church – I've let many others go. And I am much more satisfied.

What does God want you to do?

Getting off the over-commitment treadmill myself only took one question from a close friend: "Bob, what does *God* want you to do?" An easy question that, at the time, struck me as being the essence of brilliance. Why hadn't I thought of that? I had been running from duty to duty, trying to use my thoughts and plans for myself, forgetting to ask God what he wants me to do. "Show me the forest, then give me the trees." My journey toward finding what God wanted me to do began with examining my spiritual gifts.

Spiritual gifts

Almost every church engages its members in some kind of spiritual gifts assessment. A Web search for "spiritual gifts test" netted me 14,500 hits. (I opted not to take all of the tests. After all, after the first 5,000, will the results be all that different?) Obviously, people are longing to see what their gifts are, and churches are anxious to find a way to place people in positions where they can feel fulfilled and fill a need in the church at the same time.

The majority of spiritual gifts tests are based on two verses: 1 Corinthians 12:8-10 and Romans 12:6-8. The verse in Corinthians reads:

To one there is given through the Spirit the message of wisdom, to another the message of knowledge by means of the same Spirit, to another faith by the same Spirit, to another gifts of healing by that one Spirit, to another miraculous powers, to another prophecy, to another distinguishing between spirits, to another speaking in different kinds of tongues, and to still another the interpretation of tongues.

Paul goes on in that chapter to explain how all the pieces are important. His analogy is the human body; though made up of different parts, it all works together for the good of one. No part of the body exists on its own, and no part can completely fulfill its mission without the rest of the body. Some parts are strong, some are weaker; but all are critical for a healthy body. (Read 1 Corinthians 12:12-31.)

There are, of course, many other fitting analogies. If you are mechanically inclined, think of the parts of a car engine. If you're a big sports fan, picture your favorite team. If you're a musician, think of the synergy that occurs when an ensemble comes together. All the pieces are important for the whole to work.

Romans 12:6-8 adds a few more spiritual gifts, which are easily considered in modern contexts:

God has also given each of us different gifts to use. If we can prophesy, we should do it according to the amount of faith we have. If we can serve others, we should serve. If we can teach, we should teach. If we can encourage others, we should encourage them. If we can give, we should be generous. If we are leaders, we should do our best. If we are good to others, we should do it cheerfully. (CEV)

While your congregation may have different categories of spiritual gifts, most fall into the areas described in these two passages.

Your first step toward finding the ways you can serve God most effectively is to take your own spiritual gifts test. (One possible test is included in the Appendix of this book.) These tests are not meant to be a comprehensive analysis. Each congregation and each denomination often has its own interpretation. If you haven't done so yet, or if it has been several years since your last assessment, I encourage you to talk with your pastor about getting help in identifying your spiritual gifts.

Putting your gifts to use in the church

Whether you take the spiritual gifts test included with this book, or one through your congregation, your next step is going to be putting the results to work. Your results would be considered your spiritual gifts mix. Look at the areas where you scored highest, and talk with your pastor about how you can apply those gifts to the congregation. Also, take note of where you scored low. These may be areas where you will want to have minimal involvement.

"Whatever your hand finds to do, do it with all your might." (Ecclesiastes 9:10)

Whatever church you attend can make use of your unique gift mix. Some of your gifts may be used within the church on Sunday, such as using the gift of teaching to lead a Sunday school class. Some will be used outside the church during the week, such as using the gift of hospitality to host a small group in your home. *The best of all the firstfruits and of all your special gifts will belong to the priests. (Ezekiel 44:30)* By not using our God-given gifts to help the body of Christ, we are distancing ourselves from God. But we also convey a very non-committal attitude toward our congregation.

There is a tendency of many in today's churches to ask, "What can the church do for me?" Many bring an entitlement attitude with them when they come to church. "Okay, I got myself and my family out of bed on Sunday morning. This had better be good." In their eyes, the church has to provide the right message, the right music, the right coffee, the right child care, the right dramas, the right lighting, windows, curtains, and on and on it goes. And if one of those items is off any week, the member is prone to think: "That church didn't satisfy my needs. I'm looking elsewhere."

By looking for what the church could provide him, instead of what he could joyfully give to the church, this church member has lost a great opportunity to experience spiritual growth in service to others. How many times have you heard someone say, "I just don't feel connected to the church?" True connection comes with true commitment, and one way to get committed to your church is to regularly use your spiritual gifts to benefit it.

Group questions

1. *Have you ever taken a spiritual gifts test? Were there any surprises? How have you used the results?*

2. *What keeps you from using your gifts in the church?*

Don't go it alone

On a bright Saturday afternoon, not so long ago or far away, three teenage brothers took a break from mowing their grandmother's lawn and headed to McDonald's to get dinner for the family. During the drive, their van crossed the centerline and collided with a semi-truck head-on. All three were killed instantly.

This family attends our church. The mother, father, and sister, along with both sets of grandparents, are remarkably strong Christians. As thousands of people, many of them teenagers, made their way through the church doors for the visitation and funeral, the family was confident that God had plans for them, even in the face of this tragedy. The family embodied Job 1:21: *"The Lord gave and the Lord has taken away; may the name of the Lord be praised."*

> *"Though one may be overpowered, two can defend themselves. A cord of three strands is not quickly broken." (Ecclesiastes 4:12)*

There was a tremendous outpouring from the community and our congregation to the family during this unimaginable time of grief. For them to hear 800 voices singing "Blessed Be the Name of the Lord" during one of our services, had to be comforting. And when, just a couple months later at our summer baptism service, 50 people publicly professed their faith in God – many of them young people who had been moved by the family's faith – they saw God did indeed have a plan.

I can't imagine how this family would have coped had they tried to go it alone during this tragic time. How awful if they had been a family looking to see what they could get from the church, instead of a family always looking for ways to give to the church, helping in numerous ways. And when they needed it most, the church gave back.

Using your gifts for the first time in your congregation may make you feel overwhelmed. Don't let those feelings unnerve you to the point where you get discouraged and stop using your gifts. Look to other people at church to guide you through this time. If tests indicate teaching is one of your gifts, talk to other teachers; if service, look to those currently in positions of service. No one expects you to make this walk by yourself. There is great joy in surrounding yourself with others who also are learning to use their God-given abilities in new ways. You can grow together in your experiences and walk with the Lord. Of course, a strong support network is only part of the reason why you ought to surround yourself with others. Having someone else with you will also help you accomplish more.

Have you ever noticed a gaggle of geese in the sky and wondered why they routinely fly in a "V" shape? It's no accident. Scientists have discovered that in formation, geese can fly over 70 percent further than when they are flying alone. Apparently, the updraft created by the one in front helps lift the one behind – and so on. When the lead goose gets tired, it falls back into the formation and another takes over. They work together. They accomplish more.

Need another example? There is also the story of a workhorse competition where two champions were pitted against each other. One pulled an astonishing 4,500 pounds. The next, 5,000 pounds. Both tremendous feats. Then someone suggested strapping the two together to see what they could do. The result was that they pulled over 12,000 pounds – more than even their combined individual totals. Individually, their performance was remarkable; together, they were unstoppable.

> *Individual performance can be remarkable, but together, we're unstoppable.*

Along with the support and the ability to accomplish more, there is an accountability benefit that comes in working with groups and friends. Paul, the author of much of the New Testament, traveled 5,000 miles spreading the message of salvation. He could have traveled alone. But his traveling companions are well documented. Paul was a single man traveling to cities like Corinth, well known in its day as a place where one could find just about anything – if one was looking. It was a place of great temptation. It is entirely possible Paul wanted someone along to make sure he didn't stumble and tarnish his message in a moment of weakness. He didn't want to embarrass God. A good friend or a small group can keep us on track.

Finally, groups and friends simply make the journey more fun. I have traveled across the globe, and while times of solitude are necessary, the times I was able to travel with family and friends are much more memorable. These are times of bonding – through talking, shared experiences, and often laughter. Don't serve alone. Jesus could have come and completed his mission of salvation all by himself. But he didn't. Instead, he surrounded himself with 12 apostles. And when he sent the 12 out to start the church, he sent them as six pairs. Your journey, too, will benefit from company.

Don't burn out

Once you've discovered your spiritual gifts and have begun using them, it is easy to get filled with fervor to do it all. One word: *Resist!* You need to pace yourself. Using your gift can feel so good that you are tempted to give it more time than you should. And if you're spending too much time on your area of giftedness, that will affect your relationships and throw your holistic stewardship out of balance.

> *"We live in the age of the overworked, and the under-educated; the age in which people are so industrious that they become absolutely stupid."*[1] *– Oscar Wilde*

When you're out of balance, you risk contracting B.O. No, not body odor. Something much worse: Burn Out. God does not want you burning out on your gifts. You are far more useful to God – and your congregation – if you can carry your enthusiasm to one or two areas where you are especially gifted, rather than trying to do it all and becoming frustrated.

A woman in a Sunday school class of mine once said, "We sometimes get so busy *doing* we forget about *being*." Doing all the things we think we should have done all along won't make up for lost time. And trying to do everything will consume so much of our time we forget to keep ourselves in the Bible and listen to God.

"But," I hear you saying, "Karen at my church is in the choir, she plays piano, she teaches Sunday school, she leads a small group, she takes food to shut-ins, she is a greeter, and she serves on the finance committee. Shouldn't I be like that?" No, you do not want to be like Karen.

I cannot know your Karen's heart, but often the "Karens" in our churches don't understand the doctrine of salvation by grace, through faith. Ephesians 2:8-10 says: *"For it is by grace you have been saved, through faith – and this not from yourselves, it is the gift of God – not by works, so that no one can boast. For we are God's workmanship, created in Christ Jesus to do good works, which God prepared in advance for us to do."* We are not to "do works" to win God's grace. Our works show our thanks to God for the grace given us – and as we have each been given our own spiritual gifts (see Romans 12:6-8), we have also been gifted according to our level of ability.

The Parable of the Talents (Matthew 25:14-30) is a good example of each being given according to his or her ability. (While the word "talent" in this instance is referring to a unit of money, as opposed to our modern understanding of talent as a skill, the principle holds true to this discussion.) In the parable, the master gave to each according to his abilities. This is one of Jesus' more transparent parables. The owner is God and the servants are those who wish to follow the Lord. Notice that the one who was given three talents and the one who was given five talents each received comparable praise: "Well done, my good and faithful servant." They each went off and made the most of their talents. They didn't try to do too much with them, nor did they bury them in the ground as the servant who was given one talent did. The master strongly chastised the servant given one talent because he sat on his talent and didn't make use of it.

We are all given gifts. Some will have more than others will. Don't try to be everything to everybody. Pace yourself, and use your God-given gifts to build the kingdom.

Conclusion

If we are to glorify the Lord in both our Sunday and everyday lives, it must start with each of us using our spiritual gifts within our congregations. Take a spiritual gifts test and find a place in your church where you can help. Find a support group to help you through the rough patches, and remember you can't do it all. God doesn't want you to do it all. God wants you to use your gifts to the best of your abilities in service to him.

Prayer:

God, we thank you for the gifts you have given each of us. We confess we don't always use them in your service. Help us to use our gifts for you, Lord. Help us to use them in ways that will build your name and your kingdom. May learning and using our gifts draw us closer to you, God.

Amen.

End questions

1. *Consider Romans 12:6-8 and 1 Corinthians 12:8-10. What do you think are some of your strongest spiritual gifts? Why do you think this?*

2. *If you are comfortable with it, ask someone in the group who knows you well what they consider your spiritual gifts to be. Share with them what you think their gifts are. How did this exercise make you feel? Validated? Afraid? Excited?*

3. *What do you feel is an adequate amount of time to spend in giving your gifts to the church each week? Are you doing this? Why or why not?*

4. *Consider Ephesians 2:8-10. Do you sometimes confuse doing works with using your gifts? What are some ways you can avoid this trap?*

Sources

1   Oscar Wilde (1854–1900). Gilbert, in "*The critic as artist*," pt. 2, published in "Intentions" (1891).

Talent Show: Your Faith in Full Color

Everyday Life: Your Spiritual Gifts are not Just for God

"I awoke this morning with a devout thanksgiving for my friends, the old and the new. Shall I not call God the Beautiful, who daily showeth himself to me in his gifts?"[1]
— *Ralph Waldo Emerson*

Say a little prayer

A company I once worked for had been a privately held, Christian-based organization for more than 50 years. This was an organization that had prayer meetings every day as well as monthly company-wide meetings that finished with prayer. I would sometimes lead a devotional, say a prayer, or, never one to shy away from public humiliation, even sing the occasional song.

Then a publicly held, non-Christian, multi billion dollar conglomerate bought the company. A move that, arguably, did improve the business of the company. However, at the end of the first full staff meeting as part of the conglomerate, the last words of the meeting were, "That's it. Go get 'em." We all looked around, waiting for the words, "Let's pray." They never came.

> *My spiritual gifts ... were destined for a file cabinet ...*
> *This was not how I wanted to live.*

Soon the Christian icons that had adorned desks in proud public displays were tucked into desk drawers or taken home. The prayer meetings disbanded. I, too, stopped talking so boldly about my faith. After all, I surmised, "This is work, not church. We could get sued." My spiritual gifts, just like the crosses, *Footprints* posters, and WWJD bracelets, were destined for a file cabinet and only brought out and dusted off on Sunday. This was not how I wanted to live.

All that glitters…

I know a pastor who, prior to becoming a pastor, had what many thought would be his dream job. He was leading the communications department of a mid sized Christian company. What could be better for a Christian than working for a Christian company? But the reality was, he wasn't completely satisfied. His top spiritual gifts are hospitality and evangelism. It's not easy to find an outlet for hospitality in a business environment. And even in a Christian company, there is very little opportunity for outreach. So when a position in his congregation became available, he eagerly took it. Now he feels he is fully able to use his gifts the way God planned. As a fellowship pastor, he is using his gifts in hospitality and reaching out to the lost. He feels at home with the Lord in his daily life.

Gifts in everyday work life

I can hear you now. "Sure, it's easy for a pastor to use his gifts in everyday life. He works for the church!" But the truth is, each one of us can use our spiritual gifts every day. Not only can we do this, it is what we are *called* to do. God didn't give us these gifts just for Sunday. God blessed us so we can give back to the Lord every day. Remember this essential piece of whole-life tithing: It's not that 10 percent is God's and the rest is yours. *It is all God's.*

The biggest challenge for whole-life tithing often seems to arise in our jobs, our careers. The New York Times once quoted boxer Muhammad Ali, who described his career as "just a job." He said, "Grass grows, birds fly, waves pound the sand. I beat people up."[2] That is such an amazing statement. It is glorious in the way it contrasts the beauty of nature and the ugliness of boxing. It is glorious in its realization that God creates *everything* to do *something* (birds fly, boxers box). It is also glorious, however, in its compartmentalization: "It's just a job." The phrase, "It's just a job," is not one of my favorites, to be honest. When we are truly using our gifts to glorify God, every job is an opportunity to reach others and draw them closer to God.

"That everyone may eat and drink, and find satisfaction in all his toil – this is the gift of God." (Ecclesiastes 3:13)

Many people believe that to truly use one's spiritual gifts in everyday life, one has to have a job in the ministry. This is simply not true. By knowing the gifts God has given you, and by applying those gifts in your work life, you are able to look at any job with new eyes and realize it is important because you are using that job to fulfill God's plan for you and for others.

For instance, if you have the gift of administration, you could use your spiritual gift to be an organizer at work and find more fulfillment – in God and at work. Take it a step further. You could even organize a weekly lunch-hour Bible study with other believers. If you have the gift of evangelism, you could talk to co-workers over breaks and at lunches about what God is doing in your life.

Many of us are nervous about bringing our faith into our secular work lives. But if we can't be comfortable sharing the gifts God has given us at work, then what is it we are working for? Jesus addresses this issue in the book of Matthew. "What good will it be for a man if he gains the whole world, yet forfeits his soul? Or what can a man give in exchange for his soul?" (Matthew 16:26) We should be working for God's glory, not our own. It's all God's. Jesus instructs us to carry the Word of God into the world (Mark 16:15). Do not be afraid to find ways to use your spiritual gifts at work. Use them to honor God, and you will reap the rewards.

Gifts in everyday home life

"Men come tamely home at night only from the next field or street, where their household echoes haunt, and their life pines because it breathes its own breath over again; their shadows, morning and evening, reach farther than their daily steps. We should come home from far, from adventures, and perils, and discoveries every day, with new experience and character." [3] *– Henry David Thoreau*

If you aren't able to apply your spiritual gifts in your everyday life, living can often seem routine. A daily mission to answer the unanswerable question, "Why am I doing this?" Then you come home from a work life filled with doubt to a home overflowing with doubt as well. If, at the most, you are only using your spiritual gifts for the church on Sunday, you are denying yourself a fruitful work life and you are denying your family your best.

Gifts in parenting

As Christians, one of our great goals should be to raise our children to be dedicated Christ followers. We deny our families an opportunity to see all of God's blessings if we don't apply our spiritual gifts at home. For instance, if you have the gift of evangelism, yet never tell your child about the Lord, aren't you wasting your gift? Even if you use that gift on Sunday to reach the congregation, and even if you use that gift at work to reach co-workers, by not using it at home, you are watching an opportunity fade away.

"The Golden Rule of Parenting is: Do unto your children as you wish your parents had done unto you!"[4] – Louise Hart

Most of us are familiar with "Leave it to Beaver," the popular television show from the 1950s and 1960s. "Beaver" was on the air in afternoon reruns when I was growing up. It focused on the Cleaver family, which consisted of a husband (Ward), wife (June), and two boys (Wally and the Beaver). Ward worked; June stayed home. The boys went to school. The boys ran into boy troubles, especially Beaver. The dad would come home and talk to the boys, and then things would be fine. It was a snapshot of the perceived perfect American family. In fact, when I was growing up, the kids whose parents were still married, whose dad worked and mom stayed home, were often sarcastically referred to as "Cleavers." But one of the things "Leave it to Beaver" did was show how parents used their gifts in raising their children. June was a nurturer who helped the boys with emotional crises. Ward was a leader and handled the discipline – which was always practical and never out of control. Though they were fictional, I imagined Wally and Beaver would grow up happy, as they had excellent role models in their parents. I also imagined they would have good kids as a result of modeling their parents. Now, I realize that good parenting comes from a good understanding of spiritual gifts.

Fast-forward to the 1970s and "The Brady Bunch," a show that featured a widow and widower and their children coming together in a blended family (three boys with him, three girls with her, and a maid named Alice). It was no stretch at all to see the Bradys as representative of the thousands of divorced parents emerging across the United States at the time.

The show tackled a few tougher issues than "Leave it to Beaver," but it still showed parents using their gifts in child rearing. Here, mom and dad would often talk to the kids about discipline issues, but they each had unique gifts they used in dealing with their new family. Again, I imagined the Brady children would end up in happy families as a result of seeing their parents do so well together.

In the 1980s, "Cosby" and "Family Ties" came along. Again, happy families held together by strong marriages. Changes included both parents working and, in the case of "Cosby," an African-American cast. But the 1990s and our current decade have seen the "happy family" sitcom disappear from the airwaves. One of the many reasons cited for the demise of this television genre, is that it "just isn't based in reality anymore." And isn't that a shame? Isn't it a shame the happy family has fallen so far off the map it isn't considered "real" enough for television? What does it say about our society when "The Simpsons" best represents the American family?

Take the time yourself to show your gifts to your children. Let them know who you are. Use your gifts to help you reach, teach, and love your children. It will not be time wasted.

Group questions

1. *Consider Matthew 16:26. Do you find yourself toiling for what this world considers important? If so, why do you think you do this?*

2. *Mark 16:15 tells us to go into the world and make believers of everyone. Are you comfortable with this? How can you use your gifts to do this?*

3. *Do you use your spiritual gifts in your workplace? Why or why not? Why is this such a difficult thing for some to do?*

Gifts in marriage

> *"A happy marriage perhaps represents the ideal of human relationship – a setting in which each partner, while acknowledging the need of the other, feels free to be what he or she by nature is: a relationship in which instinct as well as intellect can find expression; in which giving and taking are equal; in which each accepts the other, and I confronts Thou."*[5]
> *– Anthony Storr*

In the late 1980s, the movie "When Harry Met Sally" was released. The plot revolved around Harry (played by Billy Crystal) and Sally (played by Meg Ryan). Over the years, we saw their relationship develop and grow into a romance. Interspersed throughout the movie were interviews with couples who had been together for many years. The couples reminisced on their secrets of success – what kept them together.

None of them specifically mentioned their spiritual gifts. But they did talk about the parts of a relationship that matter: knowing each other, caring for each other, making each other laugh, and feeling they were meant to be together. That last one – the knowledge you were meant to be together – guess who gives you that? God does. I firmly believe God brings men and women together whose gifts complement each other, so they can face this world with a partner who understands, who can be a sounding board, and a balance.

> *"Marriage is an act of will that signifies and involves a mutual gift, which unites the spouses and binds them to their eventual souls."*
> *– Pope John Paul II (1982)*

Premarital counseling today typically involves a battery of things. Books, personality tests, getting-to-know-you sessions – these all make up the sometimes short, sometimes lengthy process couples go through before they are married in many churches. I am surprised how infrequently spiritual gifts are discussed during this time.

My wife Jen and I are fortunate. We are similar in gifts where compatibility is a big asset, such as hospitality. We both score high here, and that makes it much easier at the holidays to simply say, "Okay, everybody come to our house." And we are complementary in gifts where that can be an asset. For instance, Jen scores high in administration, and I score high in leadership. Her attention to detail always keeps my vision sense in check. It works. Our gifts help us keep God at the center of our marriage. That is one of the best ways to assure a marriage, or any relationship, will work – and last.

Conclusion

"I just want to do God's will. And He's allowed me to go up to the mountain. And I've looked over, and I've seen the Promised Land."[6]
– Rev. Martin Luther King, Jr. (1968)

We all should desire to do God's will every day. We should desire it in our work lives and at home. By putting your spiritual gifts to work in your career, marriage, and parenting, you are taking a significant step in acknowledging God's presence in your everyday life. It is not the only step, but it is an important one. In the next two chapters, we'll explore God-given talents and how to combine those with your gifts to please God every day.

Prayer:

God, we thank you for the gifts you have given each of us. We confess we struggle with using them in our daily lives. Help us to use our gifts for you, Lord, in our places of work and in our homes. Help us to use them in ways that will build your name and kingdom. May learning to use our gifts draw us closer to you.

Amen.

End questions

1. *Do you use your spiritual gifts at home? Why or why not? Do you and your spouse know each other's gifts? Do you complement each other?*

2. *Think of someone you know with a "perfect" marriage. What keeps them together? Do you think their spiritual gifts have anything to do with it?*

3. *In Proverbs, fathers are warned not to "exasperate their children." Could your spiritual gifts as applied to parenting, help prevent frustrating your children? Why or why not?*

Sources

1 Ralph Waldo Emerson (1803–1882). *"Friendship,"* "Essays, First Series" (1841, repr. 1847).

2 Muhammad Ali (b. 1942). Quoted in the New York Times (April 6, 1977).

3 Henry David Thoreau (1817–1862). *"Walden"* (1854), in "The Writings of Henry David Thoreau," vol. 2, p. 231, Houghton Mifflin (1906).

4 Louise Hart (20th century). "The Winning Family," ch. 8 (1987).

5 Anthony Storr (b. 1920). "The Integrity of the Personality," ch. 9 (1960).

6 Martin Luther King, Jr. (1929–1968). speech, April 3, 1968, Memphis, Tenn.

Talents

Church Life: Your Talents are for the Church

3

He has filled them with skill to do all kinds of work as craftsmen, designers, embroiderers in blue, purple and scarlet yarn and fine linen, and weavers – all of them master craftsmen and designers. (Exodus 35:35)

Reap what you sew

I have a strong gift for service. This puts me in with peacemakers, the technical crew, the set designers, the cooks, the key grips, the best boys, the middle managers, the associate pastors, the benchwarmers, the batboys and ball girls. I proudly identify with those who desire to live a life in the shadows, assisting those who are gifted for the spotlight. This would include all those who sew for a living in this world.

In seventh grade home economics, we spent one part of the semester cooking (somewhere, someone is still raving about my Rice Krispie Treats), and one part of the semester sewing. Now, I could have picked anything from a wide selection of projects to sew. But I am a lifelong fan of Looney Tunes cartoons, so I chose the Daffy Duck puppet. I worked hard at my project, but it was truly doomed from the start. Even my mom, a woman adept with needle and thread, said this was going to be tough. But, being a good mom, she let me learn on my own just how tough.

I did end up with a black mass of fabric you could put around your hand. It had an orange blob resembling what could be a beak in the upper center of one side of the black mass. It had two googly eyes glued in proximity to the orange blob. Let's just say I got a "mercy *D*." Combined with the A from those legendary Rice Krispie Treats, I got a *B*-minus in home economics. Service? Yes. Talent in sewing? No.

Gifts versus talents

The words "gifts" and "talents" are often used interchangeably in today's world. You could hear one person say, "She has a *gift* for music," and another say, "She has a *talent* for music," and not think anything of it. But in God's eyes, these are different words.

> *The words "gifts" and "talents" are often used interchangeably in today's world. But in God's eyes, these are different words.*

God gave us both our spiritual gifts *and* our talents. The key to understanding the difference is that we should be using our God-given talents to fulfill the purpose of our God-given gifts. To use myself as the example again: The gift of service is a wide-open one in most churches. There are many areas to serve. But God has also blessed me with a talent for music. And since my gift is for service, not pastoring or evangelizing, I am content to be a member of the band or technical crew. I am content using my talent from God to serve God and the people.

Yes, you have talent

One of the greatest misconceptions about talent is that some people have it and some people don't. This is true of *specific* talents; it is not true of talent as a whole. There is a reason we all have different talents. Think how much less meaningful the ceiling of the Sistine Chapel would be if we could all wield a brush as Michelangelo did. Or, how much less appreciative of the Sunday morning soloist we would be if we could all sing or play just as well? Imagine if no one had the talent for public speaking how different Sunday sermons would be.

In my experience, the reason some people think they have no God-given talents is that the word "talent" is so often associated with the arts or sports. True, those kinds of talents tend to show themselves at relatively early ages – the young pianist who learns Mozart, the young soccer star who scores in every game, the young artist who can draw a horse that actually looks like a horse. But many other kinds of talents are within us, waiting for God to reveal them at the right time. Many times those talents come to the fore when we decide it is time to serve God and our church with our talents.

> *"There are two kinds of talent, man-made talent and God-given talent. With man-made talent you have to work very hard. With God-given talent, you just touch it up once in a while."[1] – Pearl Bailey*

I love what singer and diplomat Pearl Bailey had to say about talent. It ties in well with the opening verse from James that was shared at the beginning of this book. James is reminding us that everything we have is from God. Until we recognize that, we're going to work very hard trying to do things in our own strength.

Finding talent

Because spiritual gifts are well defined in the Bible, and because churches are often anxious to find ways to inspire volunteers, spiritual gifts tests are relatively easy to come up with, administer, and evaluate. However, this is not so easy with talent.

First of all, there's the vast array of talents that people possess: accounting, cooking, cleaning, singing, painting, repairing, speaking, cutting hair, listening, lighting, mixing sound, ushering, greeting, hosting, driving, strategizing, organizing. These are just a few that will be used by a congregation on any given Sunday. I can't help but picture a "reality show" style test:

> *"I absolutely believe my talent is God-given. I ask God for a lot, but I also thank him. I'm a very demanding believer."[2] – Hubert de Givenchy*

"Today on "Surviving the Fear of Finding Your Talents," Bob finds out what he's got in him to help him serve the Lord! We've set up quite the course. We'll start him off in the office upstairs where, armed with last year's books, an adding machine, and two new No. 2 pencils with erasers, he will complete the budget for the church for next year. Of course, he must keep in mind that his church wants to add on that wing for Sunday school, get new books for the Sunday school classes, add a youth pastor – and the music team wants a new drum set!

"Next, Bob's off to the kitchen, where he has to prepare a meal for a family who just had their fifth baby in seven years. The kids are all picky

eaters, the dad is a meat and potatoes man, and the mom is on the South Beach diet. Then we'll ask him to find time to clean and vacuum the church – but Sunday is out, Monday is ladies' prayer group, Tuesday is staff meetings, Wednesday has youth service, Thursday is men's Bible study, Friday is an outreach event, and Saturday? Well, just wait until you see what he faces on Saturday!

"Then, Bob has to sing a solo for the church – but he can't make it too fancy because people will want to sing with him. And, of course, some of the congregation will want a traditional hymn, while others will prefer a praise chorus...."

No one can do everything. We all have our place. If we were to try and give a talent test, the results could be amusing, enlightening, or just plain embarrassing – and I don't know anyone who's seeking more of that!

Truth is, you probably have some idea of what your talent is. Even if you walk with humility, you probably know there is something you can do that others can't. Or, quite frankly, you are better at something than most other people. This is nothing to be ashamed of. God gave us all different talents. God wants us to use them the best we can to serve him.

Truth is, you probably have some idea of what your talent is.

When trying to identify your talents, look for areas where you have a natural ability. Look at what you can do that others struggle with. Then see how that skill ties in with your spiritual gifts. This will give you a more complete picture of how you can serve your congregation. Because if you take the spiritual gifts test in this book and find you have a gift for pastoring, you may get all excited and volunteer to deliver a sermon on Sunday morning. But in your haste, you forget that in your first-ever public speaking engagement, a small part in "The First Thanksgiving" in first grade, you forgot your one line and ended up crying. It left a mark and, to this day, when you are asked to speak in front of a group, you break out in a sweat, shake, and have the keen ability to make everyone in the room nervous for you. It's not easy to be compelling when your knees are knocking. This is why our understanding in this area can't solely be about the gifts themselves. We have to consider talents as well.

"The Lord gave me talent, and I know I have done good with it."[3] – Harriet A. Brown

Group questions

1. Do you agree that talents and gifts are different things? Why or why not?

2. Have you ever explored your own talents?

3. What keeps you from using your talents in the church?

Who says?

We start to learn tough lessons early on. Remember the playground and the dreaded ritual of "picking teams?" Two of the more popular, athletic kids would be named "captains" and would be told to pick teams to play against each other. The wait was always excruciating. No one wanted the humiliation of being picked last. I was fortunate that I never was. But I always felt for the kids who were. It wasn't their fault they were shorter, or slower, or weaker. I mean, what if we had picked teams for math? Ugh. I would have been picked way toward the bottom of that one – and probably only because everyone had to be on someone's team! Who says that a small kid couldn't be a great basketball player some day? Look at Spud Webb! Only God makes those kinds of choices. God is the only one who makes all things possible.

Against all hope, Abraham in hope believed and so became the father of many nations, just as it had been said to him, "So shall your offspring be." Without weakening in his faith, he faced the fact that his body was as good as dead – since he was about a hundred years old – and that Sarah's womb was also dead. Yet he did not waver through unbelief regarding the promise of God, but was strengthened in his faith and gave glory to God, being fully persuaded that God had power to do what he had promised. (Romans 4:18-21)

I mean, talk about the impossible! Forget being 5-foot-8-inches and playing basketball. My wife and I are in our mid-thirties and are trying to decide if we are too old to have kids. One hundred years old and having a child. Now, that is faith. That is knowing God has a plan. That is knowing and believing "God says."

Okay, so we won't all be musicians, we won't all be artists, we won't all be cooks or accountants or managers or golfers. But we will all be exactly what God wants us to be if we turn both our gifts and our talents over to him. God has given us our talents to use in our congregations and in service. If you are still not sure where your talents lie, ask God to reveal them to you.

Pray about it

And we pray this in order that you may live a life worthy of the Lord and may please him in every way: bearing fruit in every good work, growing in the knowledge of God, being strengthened with all power according to his glorious might so that you may have great endurance and patience, and joyfully giving thanks to the Father, who has qualified you to share in the inheritance of the saints in the kingdom of light. (Colossians 1:10-12)

The majority of people in the United States pray. In fact, a Newsweek survey from 1992 noted that more Americans said they pray in a given week than work, exercise, or have sexual relations. Of the 13 percent of Americans who claim to be atheist or agnostic, even one in five of them pray daily.[4] Prayer is a wonderful way to communicate with God. And while we often want to fill that time with lofty, worthy things such as "world peace" or "ending hunger," there is nothing wrong with asking God about yourself now and then.

Don't be afraid to ask God to show you your talents. They can be revealed in remarkable ways. John Irving's novel, "A Prayer for Owen Meany," chronicles the path of a young boy who is, by all accounts, an outsider. Yet his unique talents lead to one great moment in his life. It is what he knew he was called to do. (I won't spoil it for you.) You, too, have the ability to make great things happen for God with your talents.

Conclusion

When Simon saw that the Spirit was given at the laying on of the apostles' hands, he offered them money and said, "Give me also this ability so that everyone on whom I lay my hands may receive the Holy Spirit." Peter answered: "May your money perish with you, because you thought you could buy the gift of God with money!" (Acts 8: 18-20)

Talent can't be bought. It is God-given. Discovering your talents should be a great adventure. Don't be ashamed of what you are blessed with. Thank God for it. Ask God to show you all your talents. Then give them back to the Lord. Use them in your congregation. Whatever they may be, they are not insignificant. Your talents are part of God's great plan for you.

Prayer:

God, we thank you for the talents you have given each of us. We confess we don't always use them in your service. Help us to use our talents for you, Lord – to honor you and to serve others in your name. May learning and using our talents draw us closer to you, God.

Amen.

End questions

1. *What do you think are some of your strongest talents? Why? What is God's purpose for you with these gifts?*

2. *What do you feel is an adequate amount of time to spend in giving your talents to the church each week? Are you doing this? Why or why not?*

3. *Consider the story of Abraham. Now think of your life. Are there challenges you feel are absolutely impossible? Have you ever asked God to help with them?*

4. *Think how your gifts and your talents mesh. Where can you best put these to use in your congregation?*

Sources

1   Pearl Bailey (1918–1990). Newsweek (New York, Dec. 4, 1967).

2   Hubert de Givenchy. W magazine 12 Oct 79.

3   Harriet A. Brown, As quoted in "Feminine Ingenuity," ch. 8, by Anne L. MacDonald (1992).

4   *"Talking to God: An Intimate Look at the Way We Pray,"* Newsweek, Jan. 6, 1992.

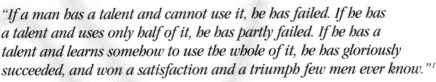

Everyday Life: Your Talents are for the Real World, Too

"If a man has a talent and cannot use it, he has failed. If he has a talent and uses only half of it, he has partly failed. If he has a talent and learns somehow to use the whole of it, he has gloriously succeeded, and won a satisfaction and a triumph few men ever know."[1]
– *Thomas Wolfe*

Uncle Harry – the trombonist

My uncle Harry, Dr. Harry Lichty, was a trombonist. This is always how I first identify Uncle Harry. Though he had a medical degree and ultimately ran blood and plasma donation centers in Michigan, Uncle Harry was my musical mentor. He was a talented enough trombonist that, during World War II, he played with Glenn Miller's big band. How cool is that?

However, my grandmother didn't think being a musician was a respectable career, so Harry went to medical school at the University of Michigan. He hung his degree on the wall, and put his trombone in the closet. He only pulled it out once a year – on New Year's Day – to play "The Victors" for the University of Michigan football team in whatever bowl game they were playing.

Does that sound sad? That's because it is. But to me, the saddest thing about it has always been that Uncle Harry never truly had a talent for medicine. He had the smarts and the ability, but not the talent. He found the only way he could use his medical degree and not have to work with sick and dying people was to manage the blood and plasma donation centers often found around college campuses.

As I was developing my talents in high school and college, it was my Uncle Harry who pulled me aside and told me to keep pursuing music. "You have a talent," he said. It meant the world to me.

Harry was sad. He had all the symptoms of someone who was sad. He drank too much. He was angrier than he should have been. He looked worn out. Would his life have been different if he had followed his talent and been a trombonist? My guess is, yes. Uncle Harry died in August of 2004. I try not to remember the sad Uncle Harry. I remember a different Uncle Harry – the trombonist in Glenn Miller's band.

Talents in every day work life

There are many Uncle Harrys out there. Many who are not following their talents every day because it wouldn't be a respectable career, or there wouldn't be enough money in it, or it simply wouldn't be practical. But God wants us to use our talents every day. Worrying about the money, or the social implications, is worrying about the world and the things of the world. The Apostle John wrote, *"My prayer is not that you take them out of the world but that you protect them from the evil one. They are not of the world, even as I am not of it. Sanctify them by the truth; your word is truth." (John 17:15-17)* Jesus tells us that we are not of the world. There is great comfort in that.

"Everyone has talent. What is rare is the courage to follow the talent to the dark place where it leads."[2] – Erica Jong

There is also comfort in the fact that God gave us each a few talents. God knew that if we all were great chefs, there would be no way for all of us to make a living being a great chef. We all possess a few unique talents that can give us satisfaction in our daily lives. An artist could pursue a career in fine arts or graphic design – but if that person also has a talent for cooking, he or she could become the next great creative chef. Finding that perfect combination of talents, that will fulfill us and provide us with a living, is a great – and fun – challenge. One that can take years of discovery.

Sometimes, it's what not to do

"Each man has his own vocation. The talent is the call. There is one direction in which all space is open to him. He has faculties silently inviting him thither to endless exertion. He is like a ship in the river; he runs against obstructions on every side but one; on that side all obstruction is taken away, and he sweeps serenely over a deepening channel into an infinite sea."[3] – Ralph Waldo Emerson

It's easy to be discouraged at times. We may hear a voice telling us our talent is being wasted where we are. This is perfectly normal. In fact, I take comfort in that voice. That voice is the one guiding me in the right direction. It is the one saying, "This is good, but look here. Could my talents be better used in this place?" Of course, it is important that we not allow ourselves to be lured away by "too good to be true" offers. That's where our prayers and time spent in developing our talents for the church will come in useful in our work lives.

Our talents are constantly revealed as God presents us with situations that bring them to the fore. Think about King David. As a boy, he was thrust into the ring against a giant, a great warrior. Did David know he had the talent to take Goliath down? Did he know he had the talent to lead armies and his nation? Or that he had the talent to write the book of Psalms? I doubt it. But David knew he had faith in God – and God revealed David's talents when David was ready and they were needed.

Our talents are constantly revealed as God presents us with situations that bring them to the fore.

There will be times we head down a wrong path. God will let us know that. Our talents and our faith in God will provide us with a truly great adventure in finding our calling in our work life.

Group questions

1. Are you like my Uncle Harry, hiding your talents away from the world? How can you change this?

2. Consider Philippians 4:13. Do you believe this is true? Are you reluctant to express your talents? If so, why?

Talents in everyday home life

Talent performs most eagerly in church or at work. Once we return home, our tendency is to hang our talents in the coat closet. But it is in the home where our talents can be developed, honed, and put into practice.

Talents in parenting

Our son, Taylor, is in fourth grade this year. He has averaged about one hour of homework a night, though some days this can stretch to several hours. He has also had a few larger projects. Fortunately, Jen has a talent for language and art, and can help Taylor make those projects come to life. I have a talent for language and also some for numbers, meaning I check math and proofread the writing and language projects. It works well for Jen, Taylor, and me. We all get to hone our talents and work together.

> *"Talent develops in quiet places, character in the full current of human life."*[4] *— Johann Wolfgang Von Goethe*

It is important to let our children see us using our talents. They need to know what talents God has given us – and we shouldn't be ashamed of them. Jen has a remarkable talent for interior design. That whole aesthetic comes naturally to her. The joke in our house is, "Don't sit too long or you will get painted." But our kids see Jen using her talent to make our home beautiful. She is using a gift from God to make our home a welcoming, nurturing place for our family.

Our children also are aware of my talent for, and my love of, music. They hear me practice guitar or piano. They have learned to tolerate the fact that I am part of a band that gets together every couple weeks just to play. We are all also affected by my being part of the praise band at church. When I'm on the schedule for a Sunday, it means I'm committed to attending one practice during the week plus a Sunday morning practice, and to performing for all three services.

I am also – how shall I say it? – an *enthusiastic* player. I like to move, jump – whatever may come to mind – while playing. (Yes, Jen supports my enthusiasm, though I'm sure half the time she is absolutely horrified.) Thus, we hear people after service saying things like, "We sure appreciate your *enthusiasm* up there." Outside of the opportunity to talk about humility with our kids, using our talents also shows them that even if our talents don't provide us a paycheck, we can still use them to glorify God.

I want to encourage you not to be an "Uncle Harry." Even if your day-to-day job provides limited opportunity to use your talents, don't lock them away in the closet. Show them to your children. They may wonder why they have such a talent for math. They may wonder why their own talent is dancing or baseball or throwing darts. Or they may wonder why their dancing is sometimes described as "enthusiastic." Whatever your talent is, show your children what God has given you. Be thankful. Be grateful. Have fun.

Talents in marriage

Okay, quick, what first attracted you to your spouse? For many men, if they are honest, looks will have something to do with it. For many women, their honesty might lead them to say something like, "He seemed trainable." But now that you're married – what is it that keeps you together? This is where lines like, "He makes me laugh," or "She supports me in all I do," are heard.

Denying our talents to our spouse is denying our true self.

Denying our spouse the benefit of our talents is denying our true self. It is denying a part of God to the person God wants you to be whole with. I proposed to Jen by writing and singing a song for her. (It has only been performed once. I have been told I am not allowed to sell the guitar I used.) I also wrote and sang our wedding song. I had both of them written out by a professional calligrapher and put into a book of handmade paper, and I gave that book to Jen on our wedding day. She has it framed in our bedroom.

Jen has talents I can't comprehend. She has such a talent for interior design that at times I can't believe how lucky I am to live in such a beautiful home – and on a shoestring budget at that! She is also a remarkable mother – devoting time to our three kids, making sure each one's needs are met – and then dealing with me as well.

We each use our talents to lift each other up (I'm the comedian), deal with issues (Jen handles conflict much better than I), solve problems (I tackle logically and biblically; Jen tackles emotionally – they each serve a time and place), and glorify God for bringing us together.

Don't deny your talents to your spouse. God has placed those talents in you for you to use in your life *together*. Your spouse is your life partner. Share your talents, reveal them, and grow in them together. It is a beautiful journey God has provided for you.

Conclusion

I can do everything through him who gives me strength. (Philippians 4:13)

We may never know why we have the talents we do. I'm sure when Jen hears me singing with the kids, she sometimes wonders why I don't have a talent for silence. But God gave us each a unique set of talents. To keep them tucked away in a closet will lead to an unfulfilled life. God wants us to use them in every way, every day. Find a way to use your talents at work. Be a parent who isn't afraid to share God's blessings with your children. Be the husband who can always make his wife laugh, just when she needs it most. Or, be the wife who pours out her love in incredible and creative ways. It is how we use our talents in our daily lives that will burn in people's memories. Your boss won't remember you never took a sick day – she will remember you used creativity to finish a project on time, under budget, and in a way that had never been done before. Your kids won't remember your job title – they will remember the treehouse you built one summer. Your wife won't remember the fight last Thursday – she will remember the time you stayed up all night telling her stories. And she smiled and she laughed. And I believe God did, too.

> *"... talent is like electricity. We don't understand electricity. We use it."[5] – Maya Angelou*

Having knowledge of our gifts and our talents moves us in the right direction to please God with what he has given us. But there is still more to explore. In the next two chapters, we will look at how our passions shape our ability to use God's gifts and talents within us.

Prayer:

God, we thank you for the talents you have given each of us. We confess we struggle with using them in our daily lives, Lord. Help us to use our talents for you in our places of work and in our homes. Help us to use them in ways that will build your name and kingdom. May the use of our talents draw us closer to you, God.

Amen.

End questions

1. Do you use your God-given talents where you work? Why or why not? If you don't, is it because they don't apply or because it would be too difficult to do?

2. Do you use your God-given talents at home? Why or why not? Do you and your spouse know each other's talents? Do they complement each other?

3. Can the use and expression of your talents ultimately help hold your marriage together? In what ways?

4. If showing your talents to your children can help them become stronger believers, why is it so often hard to do? How can sharing your talents with your children help them find their own identities?

Sources

1   Thomas Wolfe (1900–1938). "The Web and the Rock," ch. 29 (1939).

2   Erica Jong (b. 1942). "The Artist as Housewife," The First Ms. Reader, ed. Francine Kragbrun (1972).

3   Ralph Waldo Emerson (1803–1882). *"Spiritual Laws,"* "Essays, First Series" (1841, repr. 1847).

4   Johann Wolfgang Von Goethe (1749–1832). Leonore, in "Torquato Tasso," act. 1, sc. 2 (1790).

5   Maya Angelou (b. 1928). "Black Women Writers at Work," ch. 1, by Claudia Tate (1983).

Passions

Church Life: Your Passions are for the Church

Delight yourself in the Lord and he will give you the desires of your heart. (Psalm 37:4)

The kids aren't all right

A woman I know is extremely active in children's ministries. She works in her church nursery, runs a Wednesday afternoon Bible study for grade schoolers, and does various other things with her kids' youth groups, Bible teams, and the like. The problem? She doesn't really like kids.

Yes, that's right. She has fully devoted her own personal ministry to an age group she doesn't particularly enjoy. Some of you may be tempted to see that through the lofty lens of self-sacrifice; you may even see yourself in her. After all, if *she* doesn't do it, who will? But let's look a little deeper into the situation.

While this woman may indeed have the gift of teaching and the ability to speak in public, she has no passion for what she is doing. Of course, this can lead to problems. She isn't getting what she needs out of her time with the kids. Instead of feeling joy, she ends up feeling stressed. And, let's be honest, the kids more than likely aren't getting what they need – a teacher fully devoted to and passionate about them.

How did this woman get in this position? The same way many of us get placed into ministries. She was "guilted" into working in the nursery at some point, and has felt too guilty to stop working even after 10 years. She wanted to spend time with her own children as they grew in their faith, all the while having a hard time enjoying the company of other children.

So now, Sunday mornings can be stressful, Wednesday afternoons can be stressful, evenings with the Bible team can be stressful. This is certainly not what God wants her doing. This is not what God wants her to be feeling. Right gifts, right talents – wrong passion.

Properly placing passions

Your passions are the things you feel strongly about. They are your desires, your wishes. They are the things you ask God for, because he may be the only one who can help you act on them. Of course, God is exactly who you should go to with your passions.

> *Give me wisdom and knowledge, that I may lead this people, for who is able to govern this great people of yours?*
>
> *God said to Solomon, "Since this is your heart's desire and you have not asked for wealth, riches or honor, nor for the death of your enemies, and since you have not asked for a long life but for wisdom and knowledge to govern my people over whom I have made you king, therefore wisdom and knowledge will be given you. And I will also give you wealth, riches and honor, such as no king who was before you ever had and none after you will have." (2 Chronicles 1:10-12)*

Solomon was as wise as they get. God granted him great wisdom because that was where Solomon's passion lay. Solomon was passionate about using his wisdom to lead people.

In the passage, notice the things God calls out that Solomon *didn't* ask for: wealth, riches, honor, death to enemies, long life. These are things of the world. These are things that people *still* get too passionate about today. Because Solomon's passion was for God and wisdom, because he avoided asking for things of the world, God granted Solomon his wisdom – but then *added on the things of the world as well*. And boy did Solomon get it! His wealth would be immeasurable today. Bill Gates would be a pauper. But most of all, Solomon got his wisdom. And we got the amazing book of Proverbs, the Song of Solomon (the greatest romance book ever), and Solomon's legacy.

Having your passions in the right place makes living for God every day much easier.

Having your passions in the right place makes living for God every day much easier. God tells us in the Bible to turn our desires, our passions, toward him.

- *Do all have gifts of healing? Do all speak in tongues? Do all interpret? But eagerly desire the greater gifts. (1 Corinthians 12:30-31)*

- *Follow the way of love and eagerly desire spiritual gifts...*
  (1 Corinthians 14:1)

- *...last year you were the first not only to give but also to have the
  desire to do so. Now finish the work, so that your eager willingness to
  do it may be matched by your completion of it, according to your means.
  (2 Corinthians 8:9-11)*

All these verses instruct us, as Christians, to turn our passions toward pursuing God's plan for us. In other words, your passions are a part of God's plan!

Group questions

1. *What are you passionate about? Have you ever asked God to help you
   identify your passions?*

2. *Do your passions always line up with your gifts and/or talents? Explain.*

3. *What are ways you can use your passions in the church?*

Pursuing passions

One of the amazing things about spending a lifetime around music is that you see people with no particular talent for music become extremely passionate about music. Churches have great divisive debates over contemporary or traditional services (with those terms almost always referring specifically to the worship time). Fans of certain artists fill online bulletin boards and chat rooms with discussions over which album or concert was the best. Kids argue with each other on rap versus rock. Kids debate their *parents* on rap versus rock. Jazz versus classical. Stones or Beatles? Nelly or 50 Cent. Jimi or Eddie. Mozart or Beethoven. Monkees or Archies. Quite frankly, it never ends.

But the relief in this, I believe, is that God didn't have to give you *talent* for something in order for you to have a *passion* for that same thing. Those same people who are so passionate about music are the ones who make worship time mean so much. They are the ones willing to sing loud and proud, the ones who will raise their hands, the ones who will truly give the moment to God, lost in their own passion for God and for music.

> *Praise the Lord, O my soul; all my inmost being, praise his holy name. Praise the Lord, O my soul, and forget not all his benefit — who forgives all your sins and heals all your diseases, who redeems your life from the pit and crowns you with love and compassion, who satisfies your desires with good things so that your youth is renewed like the eagle's. (Psalm 103:1-5)*

Unlike finding your gifts, finding your passions won't require a test. Your passions come out every day. You can have a passion for music, a passion for driving, a passion for reading. You can have passion for fine food, fast food, dogs, cats, or even fiddler crabs. You know what your passions are. You simply may not know how to put those passions into practice in the church.

Unlike finding your gifts, finding your passions won't require a test. Your passions come out every day.

Putting passions into practice

A man who attended one of my Sunday school classes had a powerful grasp of theology. He knew the Bible inside and out. He was extremely well read in all manner of Christian literature. Since he had many strong opinions, he was a good conversation starter as well.

This man did not possess a gift for teaching or a talent for patience and seeing other people's views. He did, however, have a passion for the Bible and God, and he used this effectively by attending Sunday school classes where the discussions would focus on areas where he felt particularly strong. He provided great fodder for discussion and was well liked by the teachers.

In getting to know him better, I found out he had degrees in theology and divinity. I found out he had been a preacher. And I found out that he traveled a pretty long road before discovering that, despite his passion for the Lord, pastoring a church wasn't where God wanted him to use that passion. God wanted him in Sunday school classes – as *part* of a congregation, not leading a congregation. You don't need to quench the fires of your passions. You just need to know where you can allow them to safely burn.

There is a place in the church for our passions. I have a friend who is a true "gear head." He loves old cars and has an absolute passion for the automobile. Growing up in Detroit, I can relate to this. I have a passion for vintage Ford Mustang convertibles and vintage Chevrolet Corvettes. I am not a gear head, by any means. I do, however, love to drive. Believe it or not, there are places for these passions in a church.

You are helping draw people to God through your passion.

Gear head passions in the church? "Come on, Bob!" I hear you laugh. "How can a gear head use that passion in church?" I have seen gear heads helping single moms or those who are financially struggling with needed car repairs – and that's just one way. Those of us who love to drive can provide rides to those who need transportation to and from church. You may not get to "open it up and see what it can do," but you will get some great company and provide a true service. You are helping draw people to God through your passion. And what if you have service as one of your spiritual gifts? Now your gifts, talents, and passions are all lined up in service to God.

Pining the passing of passions

> *...when the doors to the street are closed and the sound of grinding fades; when men rise up at the sound of birds, but all their songs grow faint; when men are afraid of heights and of dangers in the streets; when the almond tree blossoms and the grasshopper drags himself along and desire no longer is stirred. Then man goes to his eternal home and mourners go about the streets. (Ecclesiastes 12:4-5)*

Don't let your passions suffocate. Give them air. It's okay if you feel a passion so strongly that a beautiful musical moment on Sunday makes you cry or applaud. It's okay if the pastor stirs a passion that makes you shout, "Amen." It's okay if the coffee is so good on Sunday morning that you say, "Wow! That's a great cup of coffee!" Our passions are contagious and people like to see passionate people. They want what that person has. Don't keep your passions in a cage. Set them free for God.

Conclusion

> *May he give you the desire of your heart and make all your plans succeed. (Psalm 20:4)*

Don't serve in an area of the church because you feel guilty about it. Serve because you feel passionate about it. Even if you don't have a talent for an area, you can help. Pray to God and ask him about your passions. Ask God to bring them to life. If it's music, see if the praise band needs help setting up or tearing down the equipment – or simply sing along as best you can. If you have a heart for the sick but you aren't a nurse or doctor, go and visit someone in the hospital. Simply spending time with people can mean the world and be a fulfilling ministry – for you and for them! There is a need for your passions in your church – that's why God put you there. And remember, your passions will get noticed. Your passions are contagious. Enjoy them. Pursue them. Glorify God with them.

Prayer:

God, we thank you for the passions you have given each of us. We confess we don't always use them in your service. Help us to use our passions for you, Lord. Help us to use them in ways that will build your name, your church, and your kingdom. May learning and using our passions draw us closer to you, God.

Amen.

End questions

1. *Consider Solomon's request to God for wisdom. Do you find yourself looking for passions to glorify God, or are you looking to fulfill passions that reflect the world's value system? Explain.*

2. *Ecclesiastes 12 indicates that when one's desires (passions) fade, the person is about to go to his or her eternal home. Have you let your passions fade? How can you renew them?*

3. *Think of someone you know who is passionate about something he or she does in the church. How do you feel when you are around that person? How can you have that kind of "contagious passion?"*

4. *Are you doing things in the church out of obligation or because that service is your passion? If the latter, what can you do to change this? If the former, are there ways you can enhance your service to even better use your passions?*

Everyday Life: Your Passions are for the Real World, Too

To boldly go…

A strong leader exudes passion for what he or she does. Unfortunately, many of us have had that boss, or seen that parent, or heard that preacher, whose heart is no longer in it. It is hard to gather around the rallying cry of a tired cynic, an overworked mother, or a weary church leader. But when passion comes forth, people can support even the furthest stretch of a vision.

In the early 1960s, President John F. Kennedy told the world that by the end of the decade the United States would put someone on the moon. It was a stretch goal, a long shot. The United States' space program was young, and had already lost several key races to the Soviet Union. But Kennedy was passionate about it, and soon the United States was passionate about it as well.

> *"Without passion man is a mere latent force and possibility, like the flint which awaits the shock of the iron before it can give forth its spark."*[1] *– Henri-Frédéric Amiel*

Men lost their lives, an immense amount of money was spent, yet the nation rallied. Then, in July of 1969, with just six months left in the decade, six years after the death of the man whose passion and vision started it, the United States landed on the moon – and the nation was riveted. Nearly everyone watched the landing on television, in awe of what they were seeing. They watched Neil Armstrong step forth from the capsule and utter those famous words: "One small step for man, one giant leap for mankind." I was three months old.

Since that July day, the space program in the United States has not been the same. Sure, I remember sitting in a classroom watching the space shuttle lift off more than once, including that terrible day when Challenger exploded and we lost our first civilian, Christa McAuliffe – but there has not been the same Kennedy-era passion for the space program there once was. It has not been a strong part of any president's agenda. There has been no rallying vision to make it so.

Our passions drive us to do the very things that often seem impossible. Our passions inspire those around us. God has a plan for you to achieve things beyond your wildest dreams. God's passion is for you. Think of what you can do, if your passion is for God.

A passion for…processed pig

A colleague of mine was on one of many flights he must take for business during the year. Phil generally prefers to set up his territory when flying: "This seat is my space. I'm going to read, have a Coke, work on my laptop *over here* – and you can do what you are going to do *over there*." You know the type – not unfriendly, just into personal space and wanting some quiet downtime on the flight.

"Nothing great has been and nothing great can be accomplished without passion."[2] – Georg Wilhelm Friedrich Hegel

But on this particular trip, Phil was not destined to get that space and down-time because he was seated next to Tony. And Tony liked to talk – loudly and with many gestures – about his life's passion, which was ham. Oh, and not just any ham, mind you, but *prosciutto ham*. (Because – quite frankly – all other ham simply doesn't matter.)

Tony was a ham salesman. A *prosciutto ham* salesman. Over the course of their flight, Tony enlightened Phil as to what makes a "real ham" so good. Tony regaled Phil with all the reasons why the ham he sells tastes better than, say, the ham in a plastic package hanging next to the hot dogs at your local grocer. Tony talked. Tony gestured. Tony emoted – about *prosciutto ham*!

When Phil walked off the plane, he went to his local deli, where he bought prosciutto ham. And it *was* good.

Have a passion for what you do

Tony had a passion for ham. Tony's passion was so strong it led Phil to the deli to buy ham. Are you doing something you feel passionate about? Are your passions a part of your career? I have been very lucky in this respect. I spent many years making my living with music – one of my passions. And now, in marketing, I get to use my passions for creativity and helping people – and I am working with artists (art is certainly one of my own passions).

Have you ever met someone with no passion for his or her career? This often tends to be true with younger people working jobs just to get spending money, so they can do the things they really want to do. McDonald's recently had a slogan: "We Love To See You Smile." So why do so few of their workers smile?

> *"To hide a passion totally … is inconceivable: not because the human subject is too weak, but because passion is in essence made to be seen…"*[3] *– Roland Barthes*

If you have no passion for your profession, it will be obvious to those around you. You will not be an easy person to work with. Your customers will have reason to doubt your vocational choice because you seem to have no passion for it.

God wants you to have a passion for living. God does not want you to toil in frustration, but to experience joy. Will every day be perfect? No. But I firmly believe those less-than-perfect days teach us how to make it through them and appreciate the good days that much more. Find a way to involve your passions in your work life. You will be a more productive worker. You will convey your passion to the outside world – thus helping your employer. And you will glorify God by employing the passion God gave you.

Group questions

1. *What are some of your passions? Are you able to use them in the work-place? Why or why not? Is there a way you could use them more in your workplace?*

2. *Have you ever rallied around someone else's passion? What was the experience like?*

3. *Have you ever known a "Tony?" Is there a part of you like that? In what area do you want to be more passionate – more like Tony?*

Passions in parenting

I have tried, with little success, to convey my passions to our kids. Emma and Grace, at 2 and 1, are still fairly young, so it is a bit early to expect them to have passion for anything besides Barney, Elmo, hugs, playing, Santa Claus, ice cream, and the outdoors. Therefore Taylor, at 10, makes a better target. Music, one of my passions, isn't a major deal to Taylor – and you can't force your passions on others. God made us each with our own passions and I respect that. Baseball didn't connect with Taylor, though he is a fine soccer player and is showing an interest in football and gymnastics. But lately something really cool is happening. We are connecting with each other in two unexpected ways – through art and by building things.

> *"The passion rebuilds the world for the youth. It makes all things alive and significant."*[4] *– Ralph Waldo Emerson*

Taylor has a talent for art. He has a unique way of visualizing things and is able to bring his vision out in drawings and sculptures. So, to nurture this burgeoning interest, we took the kids to the Art Institute in Chicago – and Taylor really enjoyed it. It was a good moment for both of us as he saw how excited I got talking about use of color and light, and he could see how he could apply these things into his own work.

Taylor also has a talent – and a passion – for building things. So far, these things have included a treehouse (I helped), the models we put together, ever-more-complex snow structures, and increasingly difficult K'Nex sets (a sort of Lincoln Logs for older kids). However, building things is not a great talent of mine. I'd place it above art, but somewhere in the lower middle. I wouldn't rate it high as a passion, either. But Taylor gets such joy from it, and does have a passion for it, so I enjoy working on projects with him.

> *Don't keep your children's passions stifled simply because they are not your own.*

Our passions are infectious. I like to work with Taylor on his building projects because he is so passionate about them, even though I am not. He got a bigger kick out of the museum than he might have otherwise, because I was so passionate about it. Don't be afraid to share your passions with your kids, but also don't be afraid to let your kids have their own passions. Don't keep your children's passions stifled simply because they are not your own. What if I had told Taylor that building is of no interest to me? Think of the fun times I would have missed out on, simply because I didn't allow someone else's passion to capture me.

Yes, use your passions to show your children how much God has given us. Use your passions to show what God has put in you. Use your passions to show your vigor, your energy, your life. And let your children use their passions to help you grow. To help you learn, love, and appreciate the fact that God made each and every one of us unique.

Passions in marriage

I was in a relationship once with a woman who had no concept of how I could be so passionate about music. She didn't appreciate my large music collection, let alone understand the reasons why I had one. She stared vacantly when I tried to talk about a song's lyrics. She actually thought of music as background noise and did not understand why I would take time away from her to practice and play music. She still might feel that it was music that broke us up – but it was really incompatible passions.

> *"It is obvious that we can no more explain a passion to a person who has never experienced it than we can explain light to the blind."*[5]
> *– T.S. Eliot*

The words "passion" and "marriage" are often used to describe a physical state rather than a relational state. I won't cover the physical aspects of marital passion here (you're welcome), except to say that if you truly have a respect for *all* of your spouse's passions, and if you make an effort to learn about and share those passions, *all* areas of your marriage will benefit.

Jen's passion for our home, not just our house, is incredible. As I've said, she likes our home to be beautiful in color and design. But she also has a passion for it being a home – not just a house where people live. There are photos every-where. The kids' art and awards are stuck to the refrigerator with magnets or hung on the walls in frames. There is a piano in the living room (she allows me my passions). We hug. We eat together. We read together. Her passion is amazing. And I tell her so – every day.

You should be overwhelmed by your spouse's passion. You should allow his or her passion to come out in whatever way it needs to. Further, you should be hon-ored that God has allowed you to share in your partner's passions.

Just as the employee with no passion for the work will eventually burn out and look elsewhere, a spouse feeling no passion from the other could do the same. Of course, you each need to have your own interests, but it is those areas where you can combine your passions that will hold you together.

> *… it is those areas where you can combine your passions that will hold you together.*

I have few fond memories of my times apart from Jen in pursuit of my own passions. But I have great memories of her watching me play at a coffeehouse on our third date. I have great memories of our decision, driving home from my mom's after the holidays, which eventually led to our daughter Emma being in our lives. I'll never forget the awesome seats and backstage passes we enjoyed at a John Mellencamp show. I can't describe for you the rush of positive emotions I felt after seeing the finished rooms Jen decorated that made our house our home — it is a memory I'll never forget. I have great memories of us laughing together — often. We share our passions. We share our lives. We thank God for each other. And we thank God for our passions — every day.

Conclusion

"May I govern my passion with absolute sway, And grow wiser and better as my strength wears away."[6] *— Walter Pope*

It might be building things. It might be music. It might be art. It might be color and design. It might even be prosciutto ham. You have passions. Don't deny them to yourself, to those you work with, or to your family — and don't deny them to God, who gave them to you. Everyone around you has passions. Allow yourself to enjoy them and learn from them. For God, in all graciousness, gave us these passions to share. God gave us these passions to show others. God, in all that God is, gave us these passions to live and enjoy.

You have now explored your gifts, talents, and passions. In the next two chapters we will look at how your style can be used to glorify God.

Prayer:

God, we thank you for the passions you have given each of us. We confess we struggle with using them in our daily lives. Help us to use our passions for you, Lord, in our places of work and in our homes. Help us to use them in ways that will build your name and kingdom. May learning and using our passions draw us closer to you, God.

Amen.

End questions

1. Do you use your passions at home? Why or why not? Do you and your kids know each other's passions? Do you complement each other? Do you and your spouse know each other's passions? Do you complement each other?

2. How much of a role does respect and admiration for your spouse's passions ultimately play in holding your marriage together? How could you better support your spouse in his or her passions?

3. How can showing your passions to your children help them become stronger believers? How can it help them in finding their own identities?

4. How can sharing your children's passions help them and you become stronger believers? How can it help them find their own identities?

Sources

1   Henri-Frédéric Amiel (1821–1881). Journal Intime, entry for Dec. 17, 1856 (1882), trans. by Mrs. Humphrey Ward (1892).

2   Georg Wilhelm Friedrich Hegel (1770–1831). "Philosophy of Mind," part 3: the Encyclopedia, section 1, *"Mind Subjective,"* par. 474, p. 235, Oxford University Press (1971).

3   Roland Barthes (1915–1980). "Dark Glasses," sect. 2, A Lover's Discourse (1977, trans. 1979).

4   Ralph Waldo Emerson (1803–1882). "Love," Essays, First Series (1841, repr. 1847).

5   T.S. (Thomas Stearns) Eliot (1888–1965). Eliot's doctoral dissertation in philosophy; submitted to Harvard in 1916. "Knowledge and Experience in the Philosophy of F.H. Bradley," ch. 1, Columbia University Press (1964).

6   Walter Pope (1630–1714). *"The Old Man's Wish."*

Style

Church Life: Your Style is for the Church

Whatever happens, conduct yourselves in a manner worthy of the gospel of Christ. Then, whether I come and see you or only hear about you in my absence, I will know that you stand firm in one spirit, contending as one man for the faith of the gospel.
(Philippians 1:27)

Turn down that noise!

For a few years, I attended what can best be described as "a nice country church." We had anywhere from 100 to 200 regular attendees spread between two services on Sunday, with a Sunday school hour in the middle. Those who attended the church were, for the most part, over 50 – though there was a small contingent of us 20- and early 30-somethings running around.

This nice country church had a conservative worship time. Generally a piano and, maybe, an organ would lead the congregation in singing songs out of the hymnal. We *might* toss in a chorus now and then, but it would typically be one from the Gaithers. (Not that there's anything wrong with that.) Sometimes there would be a solo, either voice or flute, accompanied by a recorded track. It was nice. It was polite. It was quiet.

My friends and I noticed a bit of, let's say boredom, in the youth of the church, particularly during worship. After all, these young men and women weren't raised on the four-part harmony of Southern Gospel. They were raised on the electric guitars and drums of Audio Adrenaline and Big Tent Revival.

So, to address their need for music they could relate to, a few of us cobbled together a band to play on Wednesday nights for the youth service. After a few months, we had a respectable playlist put together, and the youth pastor thought it would be fun for the group to play on a Sunday morning.

The group put together such standard choruses as, "Lord I Lift Your Name on High" and "Step by Step." We had a drummer, a bass player, an acoustic guitar player, an electric guitar player, a keyboard player, and a singer. They played well – and they played as quietly as they could. However, the people over 50 stood up and walked out before the first song was over – and the group never played on Sunday again.

The group had the right gifts, the right talents, and the right passions. But the style was out of place – even if the congregation's response could have been more supportive.

Yes, style matters in the church

It's a nice thought that every church will be the right place for everyone. That each church will appeal across the board to each seeker, believer, and curious soul. Nice thought, but the truth is, of course, it doesn't work that way. The truth is no matter how much focus a church keeps on the main thing – God – its style is going to impact who comes, who leaves, who tells others, and who gets involved.

> *No matter how much focus a church keeps on the main thing – God – its style is going to impact who comes, who leaves, who tells others, and who gets involved.*

My mother-in-law recently moved back to northern Indiana after spending several years in western Tennessee. While in Tennessee, she attended a true small country church. A church where they sang hymns, and all the ladies wore dresses *with* hats and the men still wore coats *and* ties. She has been horrified that people in our church wear jeans on Sunday mornings. She is bothered by the fact that even the pastor may not be wearing a tie. The casual style makes her uncomfortable – and has been her excuse for not attending church on Sunday. She chooses instead to watch televised services on Sunday morning – wearing her robe, pajamas, and slippers.

When I think of things like our youth band experience, or my mother-in-law's dress code, it makes me marvel at the early church that much more.

They devoted themselves to the apostles' teaching and to the fellowship, to the breaking of bread and to prayer. Everyone was filled with awe, and many wonders and miraculous signs were done by the apostles. All the believers were together and had everything in common. Selling their possessions and goods, they gave to anyone as he had need. Every day they continued to meet together in the temple courts. They broke bread in their homes and ate together with glad and sincere hearts, praising God and enjoying the favor of all the people. And the Lord added to their number daily those who were being saved. (Acts 2:42-47)

"The Lord added to their number daily." Surely these people had differences. Surely some of them preferred to be quiet and alone, while others preferred the outgoing, social side of life? But somehow, they made it through. In fact, by the time Luke, the author of Acts, gets to the fourth chapter, there are more than 5,000 believers. And we are again told of how well they worked together.

All the believers were one in heart and mind. No one claimed that any of his possessions was his own, but they shared everything they had. With great power the apostles continued to testify to the resurrection of the Lord Jesus, and much grace was upon them all. There were no needy persons among them. For from time to time those who owned lands or houses sold them, brought the money from the sales and put it at the apostles' feet, and it was distributed to anyone as he had need. (Acts 4:32-35)

Maybe our times are too different. Maybe we are all too focused on our things and ourselves. Maybe the fact that we aren't persecuted for our beliefs – as the early church was – has numbed us. Maybe we just don't feel the overwhelming presence of the Holy Spirit the early church enjoyed. Whatever the reason, we won't have a church like the early church because style matters too much to us. Knowing this, we need to focus on how we can use our own style in our own church to make a difference for God.

Group questions

1. *How would you describe your style? Have you ever asked God about your style?*

2. *Does your style fall in line with your gifts, talents, and passions?*

3. *What are ways you can use your style in the church?*

Finding your style

You can take detailed tests to find your gifts. Your talents reveal themselves in amazing ways. The fire in your soul fuels your passions. Your style, however, is truly unique – it is what makes you, you!

Style emerges at a young age. The church I grew up in had a children's Christmas pageant service tucked in among all the other Christmas services. The children, ranging from 3-year-olds through sixth-graders, would re-enact the birth of Jesus. Angels, shepherds, the innkeeper, wise men, Joseph, and Mary – the whole cast. Except for Jesus (well mostly). Most years Jesus was a doll – literally! But sometimes someone in the congregation would bravely allow their baby to participate.

> *Your style, however, is truly unique – it is what makes you, you!*

As the number of kids in our congregation grew, the directors had to keep finding more "very important parts," so all of them could be involved. It started innocently with kids playing animals – sheep, cows, goats – and grew from there. Soon, children were being assigned as the "Star of Bethlehem holder," and, of course, the well-known "innkeepers assistant." Most magical of all, who could forget the "poinsettia carriers" mentioned briefly in the Gospel of Luke? (I'm sure they're in there somewhere.)

One year, before the directors even realized it, the cast had mushroomed to a couple dozen kids milling about at the front of the church. And individual styles began to emerge.

We're not talking about talent here. Those kids with the talent for acting and speaking were given the roles of Mary, the Angel Gabriel, and Joseph. Those who were almost as talented, were asked to be the wise men and the innkeeper.

Inevitably, what happened with style was that some children emerged with "loud" personalities. They found they *enjoyed* being up front, and soon we had children, dressed as sheep, wandering to the center of the stage, loudly "baa-aaing" and munching on hay. Completely upstaging the baby Jesus.

For other kids, style revealed itself through fashion. These actors found the wool coverings of their shepherd outfits a bit too itchy. They scratched to no avail. So they dropped their staffs – and their robes – and led their loudly baa-aaing sheep away. Wearing their Hanes briefs and maybe a tank top.

Style also made an appearance in the form of shyness. I remember one girl, in particular, who was playing the Star of Bethlehem. She saw all the people and the other kids and decided she would rather be off in the back somewhere. So the Star guiding the wise men and the shepherds climbed down from her ladder and walked off stage. Naturally the wise men – being wise and knowing they were supposed to "walk toward the Star of Bethlehem" – walked toward the front of the church – then right across and off the stage with the suddenly recalcitrant star.

Those with a personal style that could only be described as "grace under pressure" – mainly just Mary – carried on. Many of the others, especially the boys, let the style of, well, "boy" take over. Animal sounds got louder, and evolved into more, let's say, "human" sounds. Soon after, the innkeeper was sneaking into the manger and starting a hay fight with Joseph. Style took over Bethlehem that evening – and made for a unique scene. Style created much laughter and many great memories that night.

Think about all the areas where the word "style" gets applied: music, art, fashion, personality, architecture, cooking, writing, exercise, hair, shopping, movies, parenting, marriage – even faith. We each have unique little pieces that fit together to make up our own style, and God has a plan for that style. God wants us to use all those things that make us who we are in his service. A great way to do that is in our congregations. We just have to be sure to use them in the right context. For example, though our youth band was a great use of style *with the youth*, it didn't succeed so well beyond that.

Putting style into service

How great is your goodness, which you have stored up for those who fear you, which you bestow in the sight of men on those who take refuge in you. In the shelter of your presence you hide them from the intrigues of men; in your dwelling you keep them safe from accusing tongues. Praise be to the Lord, for he showed his wonderful love to me when I was in a besieged city. (Psalm 31:19-21)

One of the things I love about Psalm 31 is how God's style is so well defined – it is both "goodness" and "one to fear." Many people struggle with God's style, as it seems to be contradictory. There is a belief in the fearsome, vengeful God of the Old Testament:

Hear this, you foolish and senseless people, who have eyes but do not see, who have ears but do not hear: "Should you not fear me?" declares the Lord. "Should you not tremble in my presence? I made the sand a boundary for the sea, an everlasting barrier it cannot cross. The waves may roll, but they cannot prevail; they may roar, but they cannot cross it. But these people have stubborn and rebellious hearts; they have turned aside and gone away. (Jeremiah 5:21-23)

And a belief in the peaceful, loving God of the New Testament:

A new command I give you: Love one another. As I have loved you, so you must love one another. By this all men will know that you are my disciples, if you love one another. (John 13:34-35)

But, of course, this is too simplistic a view. There are plenty of examples of a loving God in the Old Testament and a God to be feared in the New Testament. For me, this view is best explained using the word "father" when describing God. Our own fathers are capable of love and commanding respect. I hope my children would say I show them love, yet I would also hope they say they respect me (the "fear" of the Lord in biblical context is often construed as "respect"). And it is a great comfort to know that God is also our father. This is God's style. God loves you and wants you to respect him first and foremost. God is a parent. God is a friend. God is God.

If your style tends to be on the loud side – you wear bright clothes, speak loudly, use your whole body when you communicate – you most likely won't find true contentment working on the budget committee in a quiet, conservative church. You may, however, find contentment leading kids in worship time or Bible stories. Kids like outgoing personalities. The shy, quiet teacher is the one most likely to get run over by the outgoing, loud kids.

> *Be a loud teacher, be a shy set designer, be a fashionable shepherd – but whatever you are, be it for God.*

Your style is from God – use it that way

Use your style in church to glorify God. God made all of us for his purpose. Don't get spoiled and drawn into the world. Listen to God and hear what is revealed for you. Be a loud teacher, be a shy set designer, be a fashionable shepherd – but whatever you are, be it for God.

Conclusion

> *Dear friend, you are faithful in what you are doing for the brothers, even though they are strangers to you. They have told the church about your love. You will do well to send them on their way in a manner worthy of God. It was for the sake of the Name that they went out, receiving no help from the pagans. We ought therefore to show hospitality to such men so that we may work together for the truth. (3 John 1:5-8)*

We should all use our style in a manner worthy of God. Whatever your style may be, God gave it to you for a reason. Thank God for it, then give it back in whatever way you can. Your congregation is a great place to start.

Prayer:

God, we thank you for the style you have given each of us. We confess we don't always use it in your service. Help us to use our style for you, Lord. Help us to use it in a way that builds your kingdom and honors your name. May learning and using our style draw us closer to you, God.

Amen.

End questions

1. *Which of God's styles do you most often identify with? (Old Testament versus New Testament) Why do you think this is? Do you think God really has two different styles? Explain.*

2. *Have you ever let style get in the way of enjoying church? Have you had an experience like that of our youth band – or my mother-in-law? How can experiences like these be avoided?*

3. *Consider the early church from Acts. How do you think style affected them?*

8

Everyday Life: Your Style is for the Real World, Too

Creating art(ists)

There is a college of art and design in Michigan that claims it can make anyone an artist. This notion has fascinated me for a long time. They obviously have the ability to teach technique, but what about the soul of the artist? What about the passion? What about the style?

If you ever get the chance, look in on a high school or college art class and see each student's work — especially when they are all working on painting the same bowl of fruit. There will be those who capture the fruit with stunning reality, nearly bringing it to life on the canvas. Then there will be those who choose not to focus on the fruit, but on the bowl, or the table, or the ant that happened to be crawling across the table. These artists push the fruit into the background and bring their own unique perspective to the scene.

> *"Style is the man himself."* [1] *— George-Louis Buffon Leclerc*

And then there will be those abstract expressionists, whose work bears little resemblance to the bowl of fruit in front of them. And yet, all those paintings go on a wall next to each other under the big heading, "Bowl of Fruit." Who could say which one is "right" or "wrong"? Who could say, "This one is art and this one isn't"? For each painting is the artist's interpretation. It is his or her style coming through. Somehow the notion of "making anyone an artist" just doesn't seem plausible, because everyone has a unique style. It is that style that helps us find our unique place in the world, planned for us by God.

Style in everyday work life

Have you ever worked with someone and wondered about him or her: "What are you doing here?" Whether from a positive or negative perspective, there are usually two words accented in that phrase: "What are **you** doing **here**?" In the positive, you're thinking this person is capable of working at a much higher level. In the negative, you're thinking the individual is clearly working outside of his or her style.

"No man's thoughts are new, but the style of their expression is the never-failing novelty which cheers and refreshes men."[2]
— Henry David Thoreau

I have worked several jobs in my life. Clearly, many people do fit the careers they fill. Of course, Jerry would be a salesman. Yep, Steve would make a great accountant. It's no surprise that Susan is a writer.

But it was during the years I spent in music that I found myself uttering the words, "What are *you* doing *here*," with a positive connotation most often. One time, I'll never forget. A singer/songwriter/English teacher in Culver, Indiana, called me to produce a demo. For those not familiar with the music world, a demo is just what you would think: a demonstration CD showcasing the artists' talents. The demo project evolved into a full album that honestly sounded as if Paul McCartney, Paul Simon, and Elvis Costello had joined forces to write and record some songs. And yet this artist never promoted his album! Talk about "What are *you* doing *here*?" He should have been in Nashville. His talent and ability overshadowed our little Indiana studio and my abilities as a producer.

It happened again when I realized the saxophonist I sat next to in several pickup jobs around Detroit was, at 18, miles ahead of nearly every horn player I'd ever heard – live or recorded. What are *you* doing *here*? Why am I playing *with* you instead of *for* you? Why are you at an after hours fireman's and policeman's hangout instead of at the Blue Note?

It's our style that makes us unique. While we can be defined by our gifts (she's a teacher), or our talents (he's an artist), or our passions (he really loves classic Corvettes), it is our style people notice first. Are we too loud for our environment (the proverbial bull in a China shop)? Are we too quiet for our environment (the church mouse)? Are we in just the right place (fits like a glove)? God gives us our style to help us find our fit. Sometimes, we are too afraid to find out where we really belong. Sometimes, we push ourselves outside of God's plan by our own misplaced desires.

Though I have been blessed to know many musicians who were "way too good for the room," I have also known a great many who caused me to become cynical about the music industry. Take, for example, the band that had a recording contract with a major record label. They were given a pretty hefty budget for a first album, and we recorded that album over several months. Then, when the entire recording was done, I had to call in a professional session drummer to replay all the drum fills so they were in time. These guys went on to make a great deal of money — and their drummer couldn't drum. Meanwhile, the singer/songwriter/English teacher from Culver kept teaching during the day and writing gorgeous songs in his tiny apartment at night. Milli Vanilli lip-synced their way into trivia history — and won a Grammy and made millions. Meanwhile, the saxophonist I played with toils away in obscurity in Detroit.

God has a plan for your style and wants you to be comfortable where you work. God wants you to express yourself through your personal style. God also knows your limits and won't leave you out of your zone too long. Milli Vanilli fell into shame and disrepute, becoming an industry laughing stock. The band with the drummer who couldn't drum? They eventually fired him.

"God is really only another artist. He invented the giraffe, the elephant, and the cat. He has no real style. He just keeps on trying other things."[3] — *Pablo Picasso*

God wants you to try things. He wants you to find your style at work. God knows that by feeling free to be yourself, you will have joy and you will be thankful to him for that joy. When you're thankful to God, you will share that feeling with others — and God will appreciate that.

Group questions

1. How might others describe your style?

2. Do you get to express your style in the workplace? Why or why not?

3. Do you express your style at home? Why or why not?

4. Do you and your kids know the styles of their brothers or sisters? Do you complement each other?

5. Do you know your spouse's style? Does your spouse know yours? Do you complement each other? Explain.

Style in parenting

While shopping, people watching can be a fascinating pastime. Of all the people to observe, mothers shopping with their children offer some of the best entertainment value. There are just so many different types of moms out there – the yeller, the negotiator, the beggar, the doter, the calm one – all offering extraordinary glimpses into their lives.

Perhaps even more interesting than seeing how the mother whose two-year-old is having a meltdown in Target will handle the situation, is seeing how many *other* mothers are watching her. Why are the other mothers watching? I believe they watch to see what she's doing wrong. By the way, anything she does will be "wrong" to at least one of the watchers. If she disciplines her child, one mother will think, "She should do that at home, not in public." If she lets the child scream, another mother will think, "She should do something about that child." You get the idea. Parenting is painful, because your style will never match everybody else's. Got that? Good. Because that's all part of God's plan.

> *"Style is not neutral; it gives moral directions."*[4] *– Martin Amis*

The basic "parenting rules" are everywhere in the Bible. Proverbs alone offers tremendous insight. But the particular way we interact with our children, the way we present ourselves to and with our children – that is another representation of our style. And while our style may not please the shopping-mom contingent at Target, it is important to understand that it pleases God.

For example, my family is not exceptionally loud. We have fun, we laugh, we play – but we are not, by nature, yellers, screamers, or vocal displayers of emotion. But, we have family and friends who are **loud**. I mean loud. For example:

Mom: **Hi!** How was **work?**!

Dad: **Great!**

Child one: At school, we get to **do a really cool science project and...**

Child two: **Yeah, well we get to do a...**

Mom: **Come on it's time for dinner! We're having...**

Dad: Sheesh, can't anyone get any quiet around here?

Don't get me wrong – these are good families. They are Christian families. The kids are good kids; the parents are good parents. They just do things loudly. Jen and I don't. We have a different style as parents and as individuals.

These styles help shape our children. We are often surprised when our children do something that seems just like something we would do – but should we be surprised? Children emulate what they see. They emulate us. As a child of God, are you emulating God's style, while incorporating all the flourishes he gave you?

Be yourself around your kids. Let them experience the style God gave you. Be loud or quiet. Dress up or down. Just be you. And when your kids ask, "What makes me what I am?" You can answer: "Your style. And that came from God."

Explosives and marriage – style in marriage

High school chemistry did not come easy to me. Memorizing formulas is not my strong point, so the Periodic Table of the Elements became my nemesis during my junior year. I did, however, enjoy the actual experiments. Outside of feeling extremely academic in a white lab coat and safety goggles, I got to play with actual chemicals and fire. Chemicals and fire are two things high school boys can really enjoy.

We did all manner of experiments, from the rather staid (boiling saltwater), to the more interesting (mixing elements to create new elements – somehow blue and green make yellow together – cool!), to the granddaddy of them all: creating an explosion.

"Style is not something applied. It is something that permeates."[5]
– Wallace Stevens

Our teacher, Ken Duma, knew that putting this experiment into the hands of several boys could result in the school going up in one big chemistry-induced explosion. So he reined it in – or tried to. We all sat attentively at our desks as he created the mixture on his lab table in a tuna can. A flash, a bang, a puff of smoke. We were impressed. We asked for more. Mr. Duma pulled out a soup can. A flash, a louder bang, a bigger puff of smoke. We actually clapped. We cheered for more. This time, a coffee can appeared. A flash with an actual flame erupted from the top of the can, along with a loud bang that really could have passed for a small bomb, and a large puff of smoke. "Sweet!" we said. We clapped louder. We asked for more.

Über-nerd Ken Duma was fired up. He grabbed his trash can. We were already hooting and hollering. He took the rest of the elements from his desk. He displayed them to us as any fine magician would the tricks of his trade. He dramatically reset his safety goggles. He asked all of us to make sure ours were on. The flash was crazy bright. I would say blinding, but I can still see just fine – so it only *seemed* blinding. There were flames. The boom made people jump. The boom made people scream in surrounding classrooms. Smoke filled the front of our classroom and rolled slowly into the hallway.

"Yessss!!" cried the boys, high-fiving each other and laughing uncontrollably. "Well, hot dog," said Mr. Duma, a smile going from one side of his bald head to the other. "I do believe that one got away from me a bit." He giggled. We all eventually calmed down, and that was the day I discovered the rewards – and risks – of chemistry.

Fifteen years later, when Jen and I first started dating, someone said we had "chemistry." I couldn't help but think about Mr. Duma. When people say that a couple has chemistry, it's a compliment. It's blue and green coming together to make yellow. Not things that combine to make trash cans explode.

The things that make a couple work as a couple are deep and mysterious. But much of that "chemistry" people see is actually the style of the individuals coming together. The style God has blessed us with has been made to match someone else's style – so well that you want to share your life with that person. We all know couples whose styles are remarkably similar – the way they look, dress, talk, eat – all tied together through some wonderful plan of God's.

> *The things that make a couple work as a couple are deep and mysterious.*

Of course, the other side of this also holds true. Those who rush into relationships without looking for God's counsel often end up in, well, explosive situations. Interestingly enough, the volatile couple is often the last to know. They will say when it ends, "We didn't see it coming. It just kind of ended." But the people who saw them probably knew. They would think things like, "They don't belong together." "Something isn't right about those two." "What is *she* doing with *him*?" Sometimes the giveaways are obvious: She dresses in a black dress and pearls; he's wearing camouflage pants and a sweatshirt. Sometimes it is just a feeling. But ultimately, it is about style.

God blessed each of us with our particular style to give us unique ways of expressing our gifts, talents, and passions. When shared with the right person, our styles create marriages that are beautiful and unexpected. We can share and grow together. We can take our blues and greens and make yellows. Avoid the explosions – turn to God.

Conclusion

"A Christian is the highest style of man."[6] *– Edward Young*

Your style is how people who don't know you define you. "Look at that guy – he's sure outgoing." "She's fashionable." "He's shy." "She's friendly." All of these are marks of style. All come from God. As with anything given from God, we should express our style in ways God intended. What does that mean? Well, we ought to look for the right place to work, thus being good stewards to our employers and ourselves. We ought to choose the right spouse, ensuring our styles will work together to glorify God and the union God gave us. When raising our children, we need to show them our style, whether loud or quiet, competitive or laid-back, duck a l'orange or mac-and-cheese. Your style is you. Your style is from God. Use it to glorify God.

Prayer:

God, we thank you for the style you have given each of us. We confess we struggle with using it in our daily lives, Lord. Help us use our style for you, Lord, in our places of work and in our homes. Help us to use it in ways that will build your name and kingdom. May learning and using our style draw us closer to you, God.

Amen.

End questions

1. *Think of someone you know about whom you asked: "What are you doing here?" What was the circumstance? Do you know what happened to that person?*

2. *Have you ever asked yourself: "What am I doing here?" (In the context of this chapter). What were the circumstances? Did you make a change? Why or why not?*

3. *"Style is the person." Do you agree with this statement? Explain.*

4. *Do you believe that understanding your spouse's style can enhance your marriage?*

Sources

1   George-Louis Buffon Leclerc, Comte De (1707–1788), inaugural address, Aug. 25, 1753, Académie Française, Paris. Discours sur le Style (1753).

2   Henry David Thoreau (1817–1862). *"Thomas Carlyle and His Works"* (1847), in "The Writings of Henry David Thoreau," vol. 4, p. 331, Houghton Mifflin (1906).

3   Pablo Picasso (1881–1973). Quoted in "Life with Picasso," pt. 1, Françoise Gilot and Carlton Lake (1964).

4   Martin Amis (b. 1949). Novelists in Interview, ed. John Haffenden (1985).

5   Wallace Stevens (1879–1955). "Two or Three Ideas," Opus Posthumous (1951, repr. 1959).

6   Edward Young (1683–1765). Night Thoughts. Night iv. Line 788.

Experience

Church Life: Your Experience is for the Church

For we do not preach ourselves, but Jesus Christ as Lord, and ourselves as your servants for Jesus' sake. For God, who said, "Let light shine out of darkness," made his light shine in our hearts to give us the light of the knowledge of the glory of God in the face of Christ.

But we have this treasure in jars of clay to show that this all surpassing power is from God and not from us. (2 Corinthians 4:5-7)

From the least expected places

For some of you, past experiences have kept you from being too active in the church. Those past experiences may have even kept you from feeling worthy to accept Christ into your life. Perhaps at one time you suffered addictions. Or maybe at one time you led a life of crime or made other poor choices. You've battled sin – and lost a couple skirmishes. We all have.

Be assured God is ready to use you. You have probably heard testimonies from people who were on the wrong road and were saved by God's grace. These people have become very active in the church – some as teachers, some as musicians, some as deacons and elders, and some as pastors. But one of the greatest illustrations of how God can use a sordid past to make himself known to the world comes from the life of the Apostle Paul, the author of much of the New Testament. (Read Acts 22:3-16.)

Be assured God is ready to use you.

Saul of Tarsus became Paul, one of the most influential voices in Christianity. Paul took the gospel of Jesus Christ and the reports of his miracles to much of the known world. He wrote some of the best-known books and verses in the Bible. Yet, when Paul was Saul, he hunted, tortured, and participated in the killing of Christians. Saul was present for the stoning of Stephen, the first martyr of Christianity.

And Saul was there, giving approval to his death. On that day a great persecution broke out against the church at Jerusalem, and all except the apostles were scattered throughout Judea and Samaria. Godly men buried Stephen and mourned deeply for him. But Saul began to destroy the church. Going from house to house, he dragged off men and women and put them in prison. (Acts 8:1-3)

And yet, God had a plan for Saul.

It was Saul's life before his encounter on the Damascus Road that made him such a remarkable witness for God. Those who knew him, or who knew of him, were shocked to see him embrace and become the chief purveyor of what he had previously persecuted and rejected. They were amazed someone's life could be changed so much. Whatever you have done in your life, it can't compare to the life Saul/Paul led. Our experiences prepare us for helping God.

Group questions

1. *What are some of your more memorable experiences that have affected your relationship with the church?*

2. *Do you find your experiences affect how you use your gifts, talents, passions, and style?*

3. *What are some ways you can use your experiences in the church – and to serve God?*

A firm foundation

> *By wisdom a house is built, and through understanding it is established; through knowledge its rooms are filled with rare and beautiful treasures. A wise man has great power, and a man of knowledge increases strength; for waging war you need guidance, and for victory many advisers.* *(Proverbs 24:3-6)*

Therefore everyone who hears these words of mine and puts them into practice is like a wise man who built his house on the rock. The rain came down, the streams rose, and the winds blew and beat against that house; yet it did not fall, because it had its foundation on the rock. But everyone who hears these words of mine and does not put them into practice is like a foolish man who built his house on the sand. The rain came down, the streams rose, and the winds blew and beat against that house, and it fell with a great crash. (Matthew 7:24-27)

We are all human. Therefore, there are times we will stubbornly try to go our own way. Despite knowing where the rock ends, we walk toward the sand, firmly believing we will be okay. Yet, every time I have done this, I have experienced the "great crash." Every time I have seen family members do this, I have heard the "great crash." Friends – crash. Co-workers – crash. Celebrities – crash. Our experiences total up to a great amount of crashed houses piling up on the sand. Of course, the good that comes of this is that the water will come and wash these crashes out to sea, and we have the chance to do it right the next time. We have the chance to build our foundation on rock. Our experiences provide our foundation. Our foundation is Jesus Christ.

This isn't going to be easy

"God won't give me anything I can't handle. I just wish he didn't trust me so much."[1] *– Mother Teresa (paraphrased)*

It would be great to think that if we've had a life of hardship (and who thinks they haven't?), and we fall on our knees and accept Christ, life would be easy from then on. But that is not the way things work. Paul did not have an easy road. He had difficulties. He was imprisoned and tortured. Paul suffered, but he also experienced great satisfaction in writing, speaking, and witnessing for the Lord. And when it was all done, Paul was able to say:

I have fought the good fight, I have finished the race, I have kept the faith. Now there is in store for me the crown of righteousness, which the Lord, the righteous Judge, will award to me on that day – and not only to me, but also to all who have longed for his appearing. (2 Timothy 4:7-8)

No matter what God has planned for us, we have a great reward waiting at the end if we simply listen to God.

> *No matter what God has planned for us, we have a great reward waiting at the end if we simply listen to God.*

Conclusion

His divine power has given us everything we need for life and godliness through our knowledge of him who called us by his own glory and goodness. Through these he has given us his very great and precious promises, so that through them you may participate in the divine nature and escape the corruption in the world caused by evil desires.

For this very reason, make every effort to add to your faith goodness; and to goodness, knowledge; and to knowledge, self control; and to self control, perseverance; and to perseverance, godliness; and to godliness, brotherly kindness; and to brotherly kindness, love. For if you possess these qualities in increasing measure, they will keep you from being ineffective and unproductive in your knowledge of our Lord Jesus Christ. But if anyone does not have them, he is nearsighted and blind, and has forgotten that he has been cleansed from his past sins. (2 Peter 1:3-9)

If Paul could finish his life knowing he fought the good fight, you can, too. All those experiences from your past can help you move forward in your church and with God. Renowned author and theologian Madeleine L'Engle once said, "Conversion for me was not a Damascus Road experience. I slowly moved into an intellectual acceptance of what my intuition had always known."[2] You may have a slow pursuit or a sudden flash of light. Whether as a result of something you did or something that was done to you, God has a plan for how every painful or challenging experience can be used. God can use every heart – from the dark heart of a modern-day Saul, to the light heart of the giggling child, to the troubled heart of a struggling teenager. God knows what can be done with your life. God knows how to put it to use in the church. Open your heart. Open your memories. Give them to God. Let God use them.

Prayer:

God, we thank you for the experiences you have given each of us. We confess we aren't always as grateful for the bad experiences as we are for the good. We confess we don't always use them in your service. Help us use our experiences for you, Lord – good and bad. Help us use them in ways that will build your name. May learning and using our experiences draw us closer to you, God.

Amen.

End questions

1. Consider the life of Saul. Why do you think God chose him to become such a prominent figure in the church?

2. Have you ever let your past experiences keep you from being involved in church or in a particular ministry? How about in your relationship with God? What would it take for you to overcome this?

3. Do you feel you can say you are fighting the good fight? If not, what would it take to get you there?

4. In what ways is your walk with God difficult? Do you ever get frustrated? How can you avoid letting your difficulties get you down?

Sources

1   Paraphrase of Mother Teresa statement.

2   Madeleine L'Engle. "Writer, Wife, Theologian," Anglican Digest Pentecost 83.

Everyday Life: Your Experiences are for the Real World, Too

"Experience is not a matter of having actually swum the Hellespont, or danced with the dervishes, or slept in a house. It is a matter of sensibility and intuition, of seeing and hearing the significant things, of paying attention at the right moments, of understanding and coordinating. Experience is not what happens to a man; it is what a man does with what happens to him."[1]
— *Aldous Huxley*

Lessons from the caddyshack

In my first paying job, I was a caddie at the Franklin Hills Country Club in Franklin, Michigan. Franklin Hills enjoyed a reputation for being the most expensive country club in Michigan. Further, it boasted an exclusive, all-Jewish clientele – though workers did not have to be.

Since I come from a family of golfers (two of my cousins are golf pros), I was quite comfortable with caddying. Plus, I enjoy the game, and the course was close enough I could ride my bike. At Franklin Hills, Monday was "caddie day." This was the day all caddies who had completed at least two loops during the week and two loops over the weekend, could earn a free round of golf at the beautiful course. (If you don't know, a "loop" is carrying a set of clubs for someone through an entire 18 holes.)

Dan, our caddie master, was responsible for making sure there were enough caddies present to handle the bags for all the golfers on any given day. He carried a list of those caddies who enjoyed playing on Mondays – and this was the group Dan would call when he needed someone to come in and handle an unexpected shortage. Dan had an extremely nasal voice. It sounded as if every word came straight from his septum instead of his mouth. He also had a tendency to exaggerate the sounds of certain letters, so that some sentences ended up resembling a machine winding up and then releasing pressure.

"Baaaaaaab" (wind up), "this is Daaaaaaaan" (keep winding 'er up). "You waanaaa" (almost there) "earn some buckssssssssss?" (And the release). At which point I would usually say "sure," hop on my bike, and get a loop in.

Every time I would get called in unexpectedly, I would hope it was for one of the "good players." And their goodness had nothing to do with golfing ability. You see, not only were the members of Franklin Hills wealthy, they were quite diverse. Some were younger, some were older. There were men and women. There were people who were members because they loved the game and were very good at it. There were people who were members because they wanted to be seen. And, of course, there were those who treated caddies well – and those who didn't.

To make money at caddying, you had to do loops. You received a base pay per loop, depending upon your caddie rank. You started as a "B" caddie, then moved to "A," then to "captain," and eventually – "honor caddie." You moved up in ranking by doing loops. You also could receive tips for each loop. In fact, this was expected. However, the amount of the tip varied widely. Sometimes people were extremely generous. Sometimes you'd get stiffed. Sometimes they asked you what you thought was fair. The real goal in caddying was to find a fairly generous tipper and become his or her caddie. In other words, this person requested you each time. Those of us at the captain and honor rankings had established a client list, and those were the only golfers we worked with.

Naturally, we all wanted the "good" members on our client list – here's why. Between the 9th green and 10th tee at Franklin Hills was the Halfway House. This was a spot to get food and drink. Members were allowed in. Caddies were not. There was a strong correlation between those members who were generous and those who would take care of you at the Halfway House. Those who were very good tippers would often buy us a burger and a drink and even try to get the management to let us sit inside in the air conditioning. Those who were average would get us a drink and let us sit outside. Those who were notoriously bad tippers would leave us high and dry – even on a 100-degree August day.

Another interesting correlation: the lousy tippers – the holdouts at the Halfway House – were the unhappiest people I knew. Those who were giving and generous tended to have a great sense of humor, engage the caddies in conversation, and enjoyed a genuinely positive outlook on life.

Those who were giving and generous tended to have a great sense of humor … and enjoyed a genuinely positive outlook on life.

There were times, sitting outside the Halfway House in the sweltering heat, sweating away pounds I didn't have to give (I was 6 feet tall and 120 pounds wet), when I wondered: "Why am I doing this?" "What in the world am I going to get out of this?" Now, of course, I can see all the things God was teaching me:

• How to work and deal with people from all backgrounds.

• You have to work hard to get ahead.

• If you work hard, don't forget to take some time for yourself and have fun.

• Sometimes, life isn't fair.

• Talk to people. You'll be amazed at their stories.

• Being generous = being happy.

Just think of it: An elite, all-Jewish country club in suburban Detroit. A skinny, middle-class Christian kid. A wealth of experience for my life in music and business. All orchestrated by God.

> *"Experience is not always the kindest of teachers, but it is surely the best."*[2] *– Spanish proverb*

Getting comfy with the dead

It's amazing what God has planned for you. You may have no idea why you are doing what you are doing, but God does. A pastor I know spent some time in his youth cleaning funeral homes. He now knows he had to do that because God was preparing him to do funerals someday. By cleaning funeral homes, he got used to the environment. So now, when he is dealing with a family in a funeral home, he can appear at ease – a very important skill when comforting a family. God has a plan.

What a long, strange trip it's been

I am fortunate to know some great Christian musicians and producers. Two of the best I know spent a good deal of their 20s in the secular world of rock and pop bands, touring the bar and hotel scene. When I did this in college, I lived through it without making too many mistakes. Both of these men, however, got caught up in the things the world offers – sex, alcohol, and drugs.

When they got the call from God, they discovered something amazing: God didn't want them to give up their instruments, or singing, or recording, or producing. God wanted them to use those gifts he'd given them for him – and to reach those who need God. These musicians are exceptionally good at what they do because they can counsel young musicians about what lies ahead and how to avoid the dangers. They are able to show what God has done for them and how to be a voice for God whether the musicians are playing Christian music or some other style. God is using their experiences to help others draw closer to God.

> *God wants you to use the gifts he's given you for him – and to reach those who need him.*

Your place is right where you are

There is a common misconception that giving your life to God and doing God's will means giving up everything you know and are familiar with. Not true. While old, unhealthy habits will be cast away eventually, the experiences of our lives are a part of God's great plan for us. Whatever you are doing *right now* is part of God's plan. Where you are *right now* is where you belong.

Most of the people I know have a story about how they came to do what they're doing. Many times, these stories include chapters on moving many miles or stepping out of comfort zones – taking "leaps of faith." God is with you in these experiences. God is using them for your benefit as well as for his glory. Don't look at your momentary challenges as drudgery – look at them as part of the ways God is fulfilling his wonderful plan for you.

Group questions

1. Can you think of a job experience that, at the time, was hard to value but which you now appreciate?

2. What experiences from your childhood, especially your interactions with your parents, have shaped your parenting skills?

3. What experiences have shaped your relationship with your spouse?

Experience in parenting

Taylor's cousin of roughly the same age was spending the night at our house. We put them to bed fairly early, knowing there would be the inevitable hours-long wind-down before they finally went to sleep. At one point, around 11 o'clock or so, I found myself saying, "Keep it down up there. You sound like a herd of elephants." I then stood stunned for a moment as I realized I sounded just like John C. Lichty – my father.

Not too long ago, Taylor came downstairs before school sounding a bit congested. Now, from his standpoint, he was *dying* and we would be the *worst parents in the world* if we sent him off to school. We reminded him that when he stays home sick, that means no playing with anyone after school and also no extra curricular activities – including his sports commitments. When presented with this reminder, his recovery was almost miraculous. Jen and I realized later that when we laid out the deal to Taylor, we sounded like Peggy Pontius and Catharine Lichty – our mothers.

It's true. Our experiences with our parents shape the way we handle our own children. In some cases we find ourselves mirroring their behaviors, sayings, and patterns. In others, we actually may have learned what not to do, but the experiences with our parents are the only guide we have as new parents.

If you are a parent, do you remember when you had your first child? Despite all the advice that came at you from all directions, you were still completely overwhelmed. And ultimately, one line came through, whether it was actually spoken or not: "You'll figure it out."

That really is what it came down to. Don't get me wrong, there are beautiful verses in the Bible on parenting. Your parents most likely were (and still are) a wealth of wisdom. Even friends who beat you to the "kid rollercoaster" might have been helpful if they didn't purposefully mislead you just for fun. But ultimately, what happened was *you figured it out*. You figured out how to survive on no sleep and communicate with a delicate, precious being who couldn't talk. You figured out when and how to discipline. You figured out your child's likes and dislikes, his hopes and fears, her dreams. This didn't happen one great morning over a bowl of Fruity Pebbles with your four-year-old. It didn't happen the way it happened for your parents. It happened through *your* experience with *your* child.

It is important for parents to realize that the way they raise and treat their children will form the garden of experience those children will harvest from when raising their own children. It is what they will carry with them – and what will become their blueprint for their families. While they will take the good and (hopefully) discard the bad, just as you did, you are forming their experience with parenting already. Share this experience. Grow in it together. Let your mistakes be mistakes. You will make some. Admit them to your child and move on. Life is short; childhood is shorter. Our time as parents of youngsters is fleeting – but the experience of that time will last for generations. Turn to God to help, to guide, and to shape the experience for all that will follow.

> *The way you raise and treat your children will form the garden of experience those children harvest from when raising their own children.*

Experience in marriage

I believe the dressing room of the bride and the dressing room of the groom on their wedding day are vastly different places. The conversation on the groom's side is usually along the lines of "Are you sure you're ready to do this? Do you really want to be tied down?" I've heard, however, that the bride's side, along with telling the bride how beautiful she is, is more like "We're so happy for you. You are going to be so happy together." I don't know why this is, but I know these conversations form part of the "marriage experience." Perhaps they come from the experience of those saying them.

It almost seems "unmanly" for me to admit I am happily married – but I am. It seems I should have complaints about something or other – but I don't. I went through a few long-term relationships before God brought Jen and me together. The combined experiences of those relationships – the good and the bad – my mistakes and the things I did right – have all helped to make me the husband I am today. And the better husband I am to Jen, the better wife she is to me. It's crazy simple isn't it? But many people don't use their experiences as opportunities to learn and grow.

Many people will come off a difficult relationship carrying a tremendous weight, a burden they cannot shake. This is not how God wants us to deal with these experiences. If reconciliation is impossible, then you must attempt to salvage the good from the relationship yourself. You need to forgive whatever happened, admit you played part in what happened, and then talk to God about what you are meant to take from that failed relationship to help you with your next one.

God's plan for marriage is amazing. God takes one man and one woman – each with his or her own gifts, talents, passions, styles, and experiences – and brings them together. Those experiences include all of the following, and more:

- Past relationships

- Family relationships

- Career choices

- Education

- Childhood

- Hobbies

- Cultural choices (music, movies, television)

- Food preferences

- Church choices

- Daily routines

- Laundry habits

- Toilet paper – over or under the roll?

- Spending habits

- Saving habits

- Living preferences – city or country?

- Coffee or tea?

- Pepsi or the other cola?

My goodness, it's amazing that it works as often as it does, isn't it?

Absolutely. And I thank God for it every day. God used all our past experiences to bring Jen and me together, and now we are using those lessons, plus the experiences of our time together, to shape the rest of our lives. What a gift!

Don't let little disagreements boil up inside you. Talk to your partner about them and learn from them. Let these become the experiences that guide you in the future. Early on in our marriage, Jen told me the way I folded towels wasn't how she had learned to do it. At that point, I had a variety of possible responses to choose from:

1. "Well, you didn't learn the right way then, did you?"

2. "So?"

3. "Oh yeah, well you don't cook spaghetti like I learned to!"

4. "Okay. Show me how you would like me to do it."

I opted for number four. This was a pick-your-battle situation. It wasn't worth it. I now fold towels the way Jen prefers. She likes that she was able to "mold me" in that area. It's an experience that helped us.

Everything that happens in the course of a marriage brought together by God happens for a reason. In our first few years together, Jen and I dealt with the death of our fathers, some financial rocky roads, strange people emerging from our pasts, a car accident when Jen was seven months pregnant with Emma, uncertainty at my job, Jen losing her job, me getting a new job, a miscarriage, Grace getting pneumonia as an infant, and me being overseas on 9/11.

Yet, when we talk at night, we often talk about those times and how much better our marriage is for them. God knew we were strong enough to handle those events, and he used them to make us even stronger. Our shared experiences built character we would have been lacking otherwise. Each experience shapes our future.

Conclusion

"Not the fruit of experience, but experience itself, is the end."[3]
— Walter Pater

There will be more than one day when, in desperation, you will cry out, "God, why me? Why this? Why now?" And the amazing thing is, God knows the answer. And in time, you will know it, too. It may not be in your lifetime, but God will show you the reasons.

What you are experiencing in your work life and your home life is what God wants you to experience. It is part of God's plan. And as you continue on your journey, those experiences will shape your stories, your life, your spouse, your children, and your future generations. Learn from the experiences. Thank God for them. Talk to God about them. And then use them to glorify God. They will last more than a lifetime.

Now you have learned about your gifts and talents — your passions and style — and you have culled from your experiences. It is time to take action. The next two chapters explore how to take action to glorify God in your church life and everyday life.

Prayer:

God, we thank you for the experiences you have given us. We confess we struggle with using them in our daily lives, Lord. Help us use our experiences for you in our places of work and in our homes. Help us use them in ways that will build your name and kingdom. May learning and using our experiences draw us closer to you, God.

Amen.

End questions

1. *Consider the story of Joseph (Genesis 37-50). Joseph was the favorite child, sold by his jealous brothers into slavery, and then wrongly accused by his master's wife. But Joseph ultimately rose to a position of great power. How did his experiences shape him? How did they affect what he did in his life?*

2. *What experiences are you giving your children? Do you believe they will use you as a role model when they become parents? What areas would they say you could work on?*

3. *Are you now, or have you ever been, in a "What am I doing here" frame of mind? Have you prayed about it? What reasons might God have for you to be right where you are?*

4. *How do you and your spouse deal with experiences? Do you have trials and tribulations and just put them away – or do you thank God for those experiences and learn from them? Have your experiences as a couple, and before you were together, made your marriage stronger? How so – or why not?*

Sources

1   Aldous Huxley (1894–1963). "Texts and Pretexts," introduction (1932).

2   Spanish proverb.

3   Walter Pater (1839–1894). "Studies in the History of the Renaissance," *"Conclusion,"* (1873).

Taking Action

Moving Forward in Your Church Life

What good is it, my brothers, if a man claims to have faith but has no deeds? Can such faith save him? Suppose a brother or sister is without clothes and daily food. If one of you says to him, "Go, I wish you well; keep warm and well fed," but does nothing about his physical needs, what good is it? In the same way, faith by itself, if it is not accompanied by action, is dead.
(James 2:14-17)

I wish...

Feeling brave? Here is an interesting exercise for you. In a typical week, try to pay attention to how many times people around you say, "I wish someone would do something about (fill in the blank)." Feeling even braver? Try to count how many times you say it yourself in a week.

This line, or something very much like it, comes out of our mouths when we're driving. ("I wish someone would do something about these potholes.") We say it at work. ("I wish someone would plan an employee softball team.") We also say it at church. ("I wish someone would teach a class on Romans.") Have you ever thought that when you are saying, "I wish someone would do something about (fill in the blank)," God is saying, "I wish you would hear me calling!"

"Worry is not thought; complaining is not action." [1]
– Mason Cooley

We can't worry or complain something away. I believe God puts those "I wish ..." thoughts into our heads because God wants us to be the ones to take action. In the time you have spent in this book, you have had the opportunity to discover your spiritual gifts, explore your talents, reconnect with your passions, identify your style, and evaluate your experiences. It is now time to take action and put those things to use in the church – and in your community. It is time to be a part of fulfilling your "I wish..." statements.

He who has an ear, let him hear... (Revelation 2:7)

My wife and I were attending our church's third service on a recent Sunday. When our fellowship pastor got up to do the morning welcome, no sound came out of the microphone. After a few tries, it came on. Following announcements, the band and praise team came on. They approached their instruments and microphones – and that's when the feedback started. It was the typical small ringing at first, but as it went unattended it swelled to an ear-piercing, high-pitched wail that consumed the confines of our sanctuary.

I have experience in operating sound equipment. I spent much of my life behind mixing consoles, looking "technical" while twirling knobs and moving faders. I have also run sound at our church. So when the screeching began, I turned around and was ready to head up the stairs to the sound booth, until I noticed our technology director a few steps ahead of me. He got up the steps and worked with the new sound person to get the feedback eliminated. People finally sighed and laughed, our music director handled it with grace, and the rest of the service went mostly without a hitch. I leaned over to Jen and said, "I wish someone would train those guys better."

The next evening, I attended a "volunteers in action" meeting at our church. One of the positions needed was a team leader for the sound ministry, helping to alleviate the day-to-day duties for our technical director. There was God's voice – "I wish you would hear me calling." It was time I answered.

There was God's voice – "I wish you would hear me calling." It was time I answered.

Group questions

1. *What is one "I wish" question you have asked about your church? What have you done about this?*

2. *In what ways have you taken action in your church? What were the results?*

"What's a cubit?"[2]

Imagine this scenario: You're a good Christian. Despite being surrounded by sin, you have followed God's commandments. You have been faithful to your wife. You have raised three sons to fear the Lord. You are 600-years-old when God tells you it's time to build a really, really big boat. Furthermore, after you've built it, you will live on this boat with your family – and at least two of all the creatures of the earth – for more than a year. During that time, God tells you, all other life on the planet will be destroyed.

Wow. God called me to lead a relatively small group of sound people – and I had to think about it and pray about it with my wife? And I'm only 35 years old! Makes me wonder what Noah said "I wish…" to! Was he out walking one day, looking at the sin around him, and thinking, "I wish someone would take care of all this?" Maybe it was something much more innocent. "I wish I had more time with my family now that I am 600 and slowing down." It's hard to know. But God made sure Noah heard the call – and Noah answered. And we are all here because he did.

God made sure Noah heard the call – and Noah answered.
And we are all here because he did.

The hard road

In preparation for this section, re-read the story of Abraham being called by God to sacrifice his son, Isaac, on an altar (Genesis 22:1-19).

I am a stepfather to a 10-year-old boy. I love him as if he were my own. I am a father to two young girls (ages 2 and 1). At the top of my mental list of parental responsibilities is "protect my children from harm."

I can't imagine my struggle if God told me to take Taylor, our only son, and sacrifice him. I can't imagine taking two other people and Taylor and heading out on a three-day journey that would end with me knowing I would take a knife to Taylor, kill him, burn his body on the altar, and offer him as a sacrifice to God. Does that thought not stop you cold when you try to put yourself in Abraham's place?

I cannot imagine leaving the other two behind, and walking with Taylor to the altar while he carried the wood for his own sacrifice on his back. What would I answer when he looked at me while carrying the wood and asked, "Where is the lamb for the sacrifice?" Would I think to say, "God will provide"?

How could I avoid trembling, shaking, and crying as I tied Taylor to the altar and raised the knife over my head? How could I keep my composure when the angel stopped me? I can't imagine, at that moment, being able to think clearly enough to grab a ram that was nearby and put it on the altar. How do you calmly untie your son, sacrifice a ram in his place, rejoin your traveling companions, and head out? Abraham's faith is incredible.

Those familiar with the story of Abraham know that his only son, Isaac, was a miracle. He came very late in life. Every time I picture the father and son walking the dark road to Moriah, I get tears in my eyes. The son trusting his father. And Abraham trusting the Father. The son carrying the wood for his own sacrifice (a foreshadowing of Christ carrying the cross). The father put to the test by the God he loves.

As we read the story, we want the Hollywood ending. We want Isaac saved. And we are kept on the edge of our seats until the last possible moment. Finally he is. But Scripture makes no mention of Abraham's emotion. Not before, not during, not after. Maybe this is so we can picture it our own way. When I see the scene, I imagine a stoic Abraham, stone cold to emotion, afraid if he shows any, it will all come out.

Did Abraham have an "I wish..." that led to this remarkable story of action and faith? Did it go back to all the years he and Sarah had wished for a son? Did Abraham wish for a true test of his faith? In answer to my "I wish..." statement, I was given a talented team of people to teach the basics of sound to. Abraham, on the other hand, had to take his only son to the altar. God called. Abraham answered. His descendents shaped the Old Testament.

To build a city

In preparation for this section, read the story of Nehemiah found in Nehemiah 1:5-11 and 2:1-9.

Another powerful example of an "I wish" coming to fruition is found in the book of Nehemiah. The city of Jerusalem was lying in ruin. Nehemiah heard the news. First, he wept. Then he mourned and fasted. Finally, Nehemiah prayed his "I wish," quoting God's own words back to him:

...if you return to me and obey my commands, then even if your exiled people are at the farthest horizon, I will gather them from there and bring them to the place I have chosen as a dwelling for my Name.

After Nehemiah made his request of God, he appeared before the king and received the king's permission to rebuild Jerusalem – to fulfill his own "I wish." In fact, the rest of the book details the rebuilding job Nehemiah faced in Jerusalem. The work wasn't easy; his enemies taunted him and the workers tired. But ultimately, because Nehemiah took action based on his "I wish" prayer to God, Jerusalem became a majestic city once more.

If you are looking for more "I wish" stories, the Bible is full of them. Read Chapters 7 and 8 of the Book of Esther for an amazing story that resulted from Esther's "I wish" statement. God is the same today as he was yesterday, and God is ready for your "I wish" – if you are ready to take action.

Conclusion

"Is a faith without action a sincere faith?"[3] *– Jean Racine*

Most of us will never have to answer a call to action as strong as Noah's or Abraham's. We may never see results as powerful as Nehemiah's or Esther's from our own "I wish" statements. Your call to action most likely will not involve leading the sound team at church. But you *do* have a call. It comes out when you say "I wish." It comes out when you complain the coffee flavor isn't right, or the words for the choruses were typed wrong on the projector slide. We are not called to be passive observers in the church. We are called to put our gifts, talents, passions, style, and experiences into action to help grow God's church.

In 1 Peter 1:13, we are told what to do. "Therefore, prepare your minds for action; be self controlled; set your hope fully on the grace to be given you when Jesus Christ is revealed." Jesus, in Luke 12:35-36, tells us to "be dressed ready for service and keep your lamps burning, like men waiting for their master to return from a wedding banquet, so that when he comes and knocks they can immediately open the door for him."

God is calling you. Now answer. Have confidence in your gifts, enjoy your talents, display your passions, show your style, and channel your experiences. Take action. God will be pleased.

Prayer:

God, we thank you for the actions you call us to. We confess we struggle with taking action in our church lives, Lord. Help us to take action for you. Help us to think of Abraham and Noah and Esther. Help us to think of your son, Jesus. All took great steps of faith and took great action for you. Help us to take action in ways that will build your name and kingdom. May taking action draw us closer to you, God.

Amen.

End questions

1. Has God placed an "I wish" on you? What will you do to answer the call?

2. Consider the story of Noah. What excuses would some of us make today to avoid answering God's call?

3. Consider Abraham and Isaac. How would you respond? Could you go through with it?

4. Now consider Nehemiah and Esther. Have you had an "I wish" come true? What did you have to do for it to come true?

5. Can there be faith without action? Why or why not?

Sources

1   Mason Cooley (b. 1927). "City Aphorisms," Sixth Selection, New York (1989).

2   Bill Cosby on Noah's conversation with God.

3   Jean Racine (1639–1699). The priest Jehoiada, in "Athaliah," act 1, sc. 1 (1691).

12

Moving Forward in Your Everyday Life

Action heroes

I enjoy movies — almost all types. I lean toward well-written dramas, but I also enjoy a good suspense tale, and it's hard to resist a smart comedy (though these are harder to find these days). But for pure escapism, nothing beats the action flick.

Action movies tend to star muscle-bound men (and lately women) thrown into any manner of life-threatening situations that force the hero to take action to save at least himself, if not all of humanity.

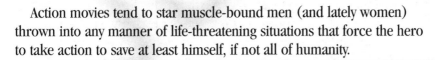

"The soul is made for action, and cannot rest till it be employed. Idleness is its rust. Unless it will up and think and taste and see, all is in vain."[1] *– Thomas Traherne*

The scripts for these films are generally way over-the-top, and the majority of the plot involves explosions, chases, gunfire, and perhaps a sideline romance. But there is an appeal to these films — the hero *always* takes action and *always* gets done what needs doing. It wouldn't be much of an action flick if, when the president asks the hero to save the earth from certain annihilation, the hero responds, "Hoo boy — let me check my planner. Yeah, see, right now isn't a good time for me. We've got soccer practice and recitals. I have a Heroes United meeting tomorrow night. And you know, I've been feeling a little achy lately — I may have the flu. You know how it is, sir. But don't forget about me next time, because you know I want to help if I can."

The real action hero knows there is no next time — the time to act is now. He knows we are rarely given second chances. Isn't it time for you to be an action hero?

The real action star knows there is no next time – the time to act is now.

Action in everyday work life

"... writing is the action of thinking, just as drawing is the action of seeing and composing music is the action of hearing. And all that is inward must be expressed in action, for that is the true life of the spirit and the only way we can be continually discarding our dead and mistaken (sinful) selves and progressing and knowing more."[2] – Brenda Ueland

How often do you remember to be thankful for your job when you pray? Every time I go down the list of things I am thankful for, my employer is on it. Not only because I am fortunate to work for a Christian organization, but also because my employer makes available the job that allows me to provide for my family. Part of my benefit package includes insurance and retirement plans. My employer provides a paycheck (which I earn) that allows us to buy food, pay for our car and house, give to our church and charities, and have some fun, too. I am thankful for my employer – every day.

Over the years, many American workers have come to believe that the employer should be thankful for the employee – rather than the other way around. This is a foundational shift in society that is reflected in many ways – even among those who call themselves Christians. These days, many who come to church mirror today's self-absorbed workforce, asking, "What's in it for me?" We have forgotten, generally speaking, how to be thankful for what we have been given.

A first step in taking action in the workplace is to learn how to express gratitude for our work. We ought to remember that:

1. We are where God wants us to be, and

2. Our employers are helping us provide for our families.

When we start thinking along those lines, we will be living more the way God wishes we would.

By being a grateful employee, you will be breaking the norm. People will ask how you can stay positive in what they see as a negative situation. When you answer, "I am thankful for this job," that opens doors. And when a door of that nature is opened, you have the opportunity to talk with your co-workers about why you are thankful first to God and then to your employer. It allows you to explain why you are willing to work so hard and stay so positive.

Ellen Henrietta Swallow Richards, the first woman enrolled in the Massachusetts Institute of Technology (as a chemistry major), once wrote to a friend: "I am succeeding quite well in my work and the future looks well. What special mission is God preparing me for? Cutting off all earthly ties and isolating me as it were."[3] We can stay positive regardless of the situations we find ourselves in because God is preparing us for a special mission. Our mission may not take us to Africa, or South America, or India. Our mission may not take us out of our hometown. But every day, every person we meet represents an opportunity to further our personal mission. We have opportunities each day to take action for God.

There are places of employment that are not open to employees who speak publicly about their faith. That is why the action step simply needs to be giving thanks and being grateful and positive. These infectious attitudes will give you opportunities with those around you. And this, then, can further your action into discussions of faith and the gospel.

God blessed you with your gifts, talents, passions, style, and experiences. They have led you to where you are now so that you may step through the open doors you find and act on the opportunities that naturally come your way. This is your mission. It is your calling. Move forward for you – and for God.

Action in everyday home life

Our school district hosts a science fair each year. Children from all grade levels compete to earn ribbons and move from their school fair, to the city fair, and then on to the regional and state competitions. Lots of kids compete and enjoy it. But it seems to me what they actually enjoy is the experiment. They are *required* to provide the "back work" to their experiment: *Why did you choose to do this experiment? What is your purpose? What is your hypothesis? How did you chart your results?* The kids know why they have to include those elements, but they *like* the action part. They want to make the volcano blow, or make the shirt clean with the winning laundry soap, or show how the lava lamp really works. Even kids know all talk and no action means squat.

> *"Action is with the scholar subordinate, but it is essential. Without it, he is not yet man. Without it, thought can never ripen into truth."*[4] *– Ralph Waldo Emerson*

Action in parenting

Let's start with an easy one. Do you pray with your children? I think most Christian parents have some sort of prayer time with their children (outside of the blessing at the dinner table). Usually at night, or maybe first thing in the morning, it is the "things we're thankful for" and "people to pray for" prayer. It is also a time for you and your child (or children) to go before the Lord together.

> *"Action without a name, a "who" attached to it, is meaningless."*[5] *— Hannah Arendt*

Here's one that's a little tougher. Do you read, study, or do a devotional from the Bible with your children? I think many Christian parents have some type of Bible time with their children, though probably fewer than those who pray. Far too many rely on Sunday school to provide that part of their children's education. Sunday school is one hour per week. There are 168 hours in a week. Who is influencing your children the other 167? If you read and study the Bible with your children every day, it is another chance for them to see you spending time with them and the Lord.

Okay, now the really tough one. How do your children see you living the faith you claim? Do they see you pray at night with them, read a devotional with them – and then hear you and your spouse argue frequently? Do they listen when you tell them to give a part of their allowance to charity, yet wonder why you put so little in the offering plate, walk past the beggar, and ignore the red kettle? Do they hear you say how vital it is to be honest, and how church is extremely important, yet listen as you make up an excuse on the phone about why you can't help with an event?

Look at yourself through the eyes of your child. Do your actions match your words? Yes, pray with your children. Yes, spend time in the Word with your children. But don't drop the ball there – don't forget about living what you say you believe. Don't just go through the motions. Show your children what living as a Christian means. Let the eyes of your child hold you accountable. Remember, all talk and no action means squat.

Action in marriage

I believe in serving others – and it starts with my family. For me, that means Jen. Don't get me wrong, we are partners through and through, but to love without action is to let the love go dormant. The quote from Sarah Patton Boyle is fitting in this chapter. For service can be serving the poor in Rwanda, painting the church, helping my kids with their homework, or giving Jen a day of rest.

> *"Service ... is love in action, love 'made flesh'; service is the body, the incarnation of love. Love is the impetus, service the act, and creativity the result with many by-products."*[6] *– Sarah Patton Boyle*

My wife is higher on my prayer list than my employer is – a lot higher. I am thankful for Jen every day, and even though she knows this, I tell her every day. This is action in marriage. Marriages fail in alarming numbers today. Jen and I have both survived prior attempts, ever grateful to God for bringing us together now. There are countless books on marriage and why so many fail. Here is my theory: People aren't joining in Christian marriages – and even when they do, many of us are all talk and no action.

Yet, men are amazing when dating. The true hunter in us comes out. We see what we want and we spare no expense or shame to get it. We dazzle with flowers and notes and poems and gifts. We see movies we wouldn't ever go to with "the guys." We cook dinner. We take dancing lessons. We shop. We buy a ring. We plan an elaborate proposal. We get through the wedding.

Then we become husbands and, eventually, our actions stop. Maybe over time, maybe as a natural "fallback" position, since we're no longer in hot pursuit of our prize. The words, "I love you" are still said, but he doesn't take her out anymore. She still says, "I love you," but no longer leaves notes in his lunch. What about the words, "I'm *in* love with you?" Action. You don't just love, you are in love.

Think about what a wonderful gift your spouse is. Think about what a wonderful gift from God love is. God brings two people together to grow in love and grow together in what God has given them. God has never been one to just sit back on his laurels. Neither should you.

Show your spouse you are thankful to God for him or her. *Tell* your spouse you are thankful for him or her. *Shout it* from the windows. Grab your spouse and dance with her – in front of the kids – to express your thankfulness. Hold your spouse's hand in public so everyone will know you are thankful.

And finally, pray with your spouse, so God will know you are thankful. Don't take this person for granted. Don't let your love lie dormant. Be a servant. Put your love into action. Show your spouse you don't just love, but you are in love.

Group questions

1. *Are you thankful for your employer? Why or why not? How could you be more thankful? Will it make a difference in your attitude at work to be thankful?*

2. *Do you pray with your children? Do you read the Bible with them? Do your children see you taking action in life or are you just going through the motions?*

3. *In what ways do you serve your spouse? Does your spouse know how much he or she means to you? In what ways do you show this?*

Protocol, alcohol, and Geritol[7]

My father was an alcoholic. After he and my mother divorced in 1974 (I was five), Dad went to Alcoholics Anonymous and got sober. He had already been divorced once before and didn't get to see his three kids from that marriage very often. He didn't want that to happen with me. A crisis of emotion caused action.

For 20 of my most formative years, Dad was clean. He picked me up every other weekend. We golfed, we went to church, we went to northern Michigan on vacations. We attended jazz concerts and classical performances. Dad came to my concerts, and he came to some sporting events (he even stood in the sleet and rain to see me run cross-country – not exactly a spectator sport). He remarried.

I was a senior in high school when Dad and his third wife divorced. She called me, asked me to meet her for breakfast, and told me she was leaving my father. She did her best to explain to me the circumstances and was really looking for my approval. I told her I mostly understood, which was the most honest I could be at the time.

During my time in college, Dad went through some rough times. After making a move to Midland, Michigan, he finally got back on his feet. He started working as a starter at the local country club (See? We *are* a golfing family.) and teaching business courses at the local college. He even met a lady and developed a relationship.

In 1994, a friend and I met Dad and his lady friend at the Detroit Jazz Festival and had dinner afterward. Dad ordered a glass of wine with dinner. Then another – and another. After dinner, as we were heading to our car, my friend, who knew my family history, asked about Dad's wine. I, too, had been caught off guard.

Apparently, while staying with my aunt and uncle during a tough time, Dad had started having a glass of wine with them at dinner. It didn't take long. Over the next few years, his drinking elevated again to staggering levels – moving from wine to his preferred Scotch. At the peak of his climb, his lady friend told him he would have to decide between her or the alcohol, a place Dad had been before. The morning he decided to tell her he would try to quit, she was found dead in her apartment. That was the end of his effort to stay sober.

Alcohol became Dad's passion. And I was soon getting calls at all hours of the night from him – during which I'd do everything from talking him down from suicidal rants to explaining how to balance his checkbook. I would go and see him and find he was fading away. He would have his meals delivered, but he wouldn't eat. He couldn't drive because he had been in jail for DUI (driving under the influence). His license had been revoked, then his car repossessed. ("What did you learn, Dad?" "Drive first – then do your drinking.") The money I sent to get him out of a jam on his rent went to alcohol – after that I sent it directly to the apartment complex. I got Dad into the best rehabilitation center in Michigan. He walked out after two days.

Soon, I started getting calls weekly – then even more frequently – from the hospital where he would go and try to dry out for a few days. Finally, on Sept. 12, 2000, I got the call from the hospital that said, "You need to come up here." Dad had slipped and fallen while walking home from the liquor store. He had so much alcohol in his bloodstream the blood couldn't clot, and it caused brain damage. On Sept. 13, 2000, my dad's 70th birthday, I stood in a cold, white hospital room and watched as the nurses and the doctor pulled the plug on Dad's life support. I held his hand as the machines showed his heart stopping. I looked at the frail body that I once saw as so strong. I looked at the messy, unshaven face of a man who was once so handsome. I cried for so many reasons, but mainly because it didn't seem it should end this way.

Our actions affect our lives. My dad's action when I was five (getting sober) led to us having a very strong father/son relationship. During that time, my father was able to warn me about the dangers of alcohol. He was able to tell one of my older brothers to be careful with drinking when he went to college. He was strong and fit – we would golf, walk, swim, bowl, play football, baseball, and basketball with no problems. His mind was sharp – he was a terrific joke and storyteller. He was my dad. And I was his son.

Dad's actions late in life (returning to alcohol) led to his brothers and sisters going into denial and finally dismissing him. It led to my older sisters writing him off. It cost me many sleepless nights and was one of the factors in the demise of my short-lived first marriage. Dad was unhealthy. His mind was not what it was. A passion for reading had eroded into hours in front of the television with a glass in one hand and a cigarette in the other. He wasn't the dad I knew. But I was still his son.

I couldn't force my dad to take action, nor can this book force you to. But God has blessed you with gifts, talents, passions, a style, and experiences that he wants you to use. Take action in your life. Take action *for good*. Your actions will affect far more than just you. They will affect those around you and last beyond your lifetime. It is time to heed your call.

Conclusion

"Action from principle, the perception and the performance of right, changes things and relations; it is essentially revolutionary, and does not consist wholly with anything which was. It not only divides States and churches, it divides families; ay, it divides the individual, separating the diabolical in him from the divine."[8] *– Henry David Thoreau*

I can think of few things sadder than knowing your gifts, developing your talents, recognizing your passions, possessing a unique style, and living through life's experiences – but taking no action with them. God gave us all these things so we could take action, so we could be empowered to reach those at work. He gave us all these things to help us reach our children and to serve our spouse. But most of all, God gave us these things to serve him. What a glorious mission! What a glorious calling. Your actions will reach beyond your lifetime – and may reach for generations. They may only reach as far as your son, or daughter, or neighbor. But they will reach. And someday you can look at your life and say, "I was more than mere words; I was action. I heard and I answered. And I am forever grateful and forever thankful to my God."

Prayer:

God, we thank you for the actions you call us to. We confess we struggle with taking action in our everyday lives, Lord. Help us to take action for you. Help us to think of your son, Jesus, who took great steps of faith and took great action for you. Help us to take action in ways that will build your name and kingdom. May taking action draw us closer to you, God.

Amen.

End questions

1. *Have you had someone like my dad in your life? How did it affect you? What actions did you take?*

2. *What is a course of action you have taken in your everyday life? Has it been successful?*

3. *As a group, can you come up with five ways to take action for Christ in your everyday lives?*

Sources

1   Thomas Traherne (1636–1674). "Fourth Century," no. 95, "Centuries" (1908).

2   Brenda Ueland (1891–1985). "Me," ch. 8 (1939).

3   Ellen Henrietta Swallow Richards (1842–1911). As quoted in "The Life of Ellen H. Richards," ch. 5, by Caroline L. Hunt (1912).

4   Ralph Waldo Emerson (1803–1882). Oration, August 31, 1837, delivered before the Phi Beta Kappa Society, Cambridge, Massachusetts. "The American Scholar," repr. in "Emerson: Essays and Lectures," ed. Joel Porte (1983).

5   Hannah Arendt (1906–1975). "*Action*," ch. 24, "The Human Condition" (1958).

6   Sarah Patton Boyle. "The Desegregated Heart," part 3, ch. 3 (1962).

7   Adlai Ewing Stevenson (1900–65). Definition of diplomatic life – Herbert J. Muller, Adlai Stevenson, p. 274 (1967).

8   Henry David Thoreau (1817–1862). "*Civil Disobedience*," originally published as "*Resistance to Civil Government*" (1849), in "The Writings of Henry David Thoreau," vol. 4, p. 367, Houghton Mifflin (1906).

Final Word: The Other Side

"Our deepest fear is not that we are inadequate. Our deepest fear is that we are powerful beyond measure. It is our light, not our darkness that most frightens us. We ask ourselves, 'Who am I to be brilliant, gorgeous, talented, and fabulous?' Actually, who are you not to be? You are a child of God. Your playing small doesn't serve the world. There's nothing enlightened about shrinking so that other people won't feel insecure around you. We were born to manifest the glory of God that is within us. And as we let our own light shine, we unconsciously give other people permission to do the same. As we are liberated from our own fear, our presence automatically liberates others."
– Nelson Mandela

It's not always easy to focus on our strengths, as the quote from Nelson Mandela suggests. On the other hand, most of us are quite adept – and strangely, more comfortable – focusing on the areas where we struggle or are lacking. For instance, there is no debating that I am mechanically challenged. I can't sing or play a musical instrument. And though I feel compassion, my mercy gifts are weak, so in a time of need there are many others you would rather have at your side. These things about myself I know and accept.

But I also know what I am good at. Accepting *that* is not so easy. Why? Sometimes the struggle is forced humility. We remember Paul saying, "Do not think of yourself more highly than you ought," (Romans 12:3) but we misunderstand his intent and overcompensate. Paul didn't say we are to think *lowly* of ourselves – just not *too* highly. We are amazing creations – made in the image of our holy God and made to be his witnesses to the world. That's a high calling!

I recall what my colleague, Lynn Miller, often asks in response to someone who is downplaying his or her special God-given qualities: "Did God make a mistake with you?" I don't think so. There are no mistakes with God. Though I wish I could sing or fix my car engine, I can't. But there are people who can do those things. And as for me, I can teach; I can lead and organize ideas; I can encourage and exhort. That's my giftedness. All of it comprised of perfect gifts from the Father (James 1:17).

Talent Show: Your Faith in Full Color, has hopefully shown you how to embrace what makes you unique and how God can use you — yes, even you — in his infinite plan. As Bob Lichty has pointed out, using our talents and passions for God is not just a Sunday morning activity. It's 24/7. For a lifetime. You were "born to manifest the glory of God!" What could be more God-honoring than embracing how you've been created to bring glory and praise to the Creator himself?

— Steve Ganger, MMA Director of Stewardship Education

Talent Show: Your Faith in Full Color

Spiritual Gifts Test[1]

Overview

A gifts test begins with the knowledge that we all have gifts that are necessary to the work of God. We do not all have the same gifts, we each offer something unique to Christ's service. No gift is better than another. They are all precious from God. All gifts are needed in the life of the church.

> "We must learn always to find and procure the advantage of God. For God does not give gifts, nor did he ever give one, so that we might keep it and take satisfaction in it; but all were given – all he ever gave on earth or in heaven – that he might give this one more: himself. Therefore I say that we must learn to look through every gift and every event to God and never be content with the thing itself. There is no stopping place in this life – no, nor was there ever one, no matter how far away a person had gone. This above all, then, be ready at all times for the gifts of God and always for new ones."[2] – Johanes Eckhart

It is helpful to test one's ministry against the fruits of the spirit listed in Galatians: "By contrast, the fruit of the Spirit is love, joy, peace, patience, kindness, generosity, faithfulness, gentleness, and self-control."

Your ministry should be fruitful. If one has the gift of teaching then preparing for a class should bring forth feelings of love, joy, peace, etc. as opposed to making one feel anxious, impatient, or imposed upon.

To take the Spiritual Gifts Test, answer each question. After you have taken the whole test, note your answers on the Spiritual Gifts Profile Sheet (Part one). Then list your gifts in descending order on the Spiritual Gifts Profile Sheet (Part two), noting the score and interpret the results using the List of Spiritual Gifts (p. 182). Some questions to consider would be:

- Do I agree with the results? Why or why not?

- Am I using my strongest gifts? What do I need to do differently?

- Are there gifts I would like to make stronger? How would I do that?

- What does this exercise lead me to do now?

Discerning one's gifts should not be done alone. It is strongly recommended you make a copy of the test and have someone who knows you well (spouse, best friend, child) take it thinking of you. By comparing these results you can eliminate anomalies and perhaps find a new perspective on yourself.

If you are in a small group, this can be a group exercise where affirmations can be made while sharing results. The group should feel free to discuss the results openly. If there are surprises, they can be shared. If there are doubts, the group can humbly discuss them and look for feedback, support and/or clarification.

Instructions

Time: 15-20 minutes

1. There are a total of 105 statements below. Circle whether you Strongly Agree, Agree Somewhat, are Undecided, Disagree Somewhat, or Strongly Disagree with each question. Don't be modest; answer spontaneously and honestly.

2. After you have taken the test, transfer the number value of each of your answers onto the space provided on the Spiritual Gifts Profile Sheet (Part one).

3. Total your scores for each of the gifts. Each gift will have a score between zero and 20.

4. Order the gifts in descending order of score, one on each line, in the Spiritual Gifts Profile Sheet (Part two). Higher scores indicate your more dominant gifts.

5. Use the List of Spiritual Gifts for further study and review the questions above.

The test

	Strongly Agree	Agree Somewhat	Undecided	Disagree Somewhat	Strongly Disagree
1. I find great joy in leading people to accomplish group goals.	4	3	2	1	0
2. I feel called to be a leader in the church.	4	3	2	1	0
3. I look for opportunities to assist people who have trouble fending for themselves.	4	3	2	1	0
4. It is easy to perceive if what a person is doing is honest or dishonest.	4	3	2	1	0
5. I enjoy sharing about God with people who are not church-goers.	4	3	2	1	0
6. I enjoy motivating people to a higher spiritual commitment.	4	3	2	1	0

	Strongly Agree	Agree Somewhat	Undecided	Disagree Somewhat	Strongly Disagree
7. I try to do God's will, even when it is not the popular thing to do.	4	3	2	1	0
8. It is very satisfying to give generously of my money for God's work.	4	3	2	1	0
9. I enjoy the opportunity to pray with and for a person who is physically ill.	4	3	2	1	0
10. I like having people in my home.	4	3	2	1	0
11. I seem to instinctively recognize prayer needs.	4	3	2	1	0
12. I enjoy learning new things.	4	3	2	1	0
13. I feel great compassion for the problems of others.	4	3	2	1	0
14. I adapt easily in a culture different from my own.	4	3	2	1	0
15. I enjoy having the responsibility of leading other people in their spiritual lives.	4	3	2	1	0
16. Because I have great trust in God I am ready to try the impossible.	4	3	2	1	0
17. I like to talk about spirituality with other Christians.	4	3	2	1	0
18. I enjoy doing "chores" around the church.	4	3	2	1	0
19. I am excited to help people discover important insights into the scriptures.	4	3	2	1	0
20. I communicate easily with people of a different cultural or language background.	4	3	2	1	0
21. People with spiritual problems have come to me for counsel.	4	3	2	1	0
22. People enjoy following my leadership when undertaking an important task.	4	3	2	1	0
23. I feel that God grants me wisdom to lead people in spiritual matters.	4	3	2	1	0
24. I enjoy helping with emergency tasks around the church.	4	3	2	1	0
25. I have a sense of the direction in which God is leading me.	4	3	2	1	0
26. I can sense when the Holy Spirit is leading a person to accept Christ into their life.	4	3	2	1	0
27. I have a knack for bringing out the best in others.	4	3	2	1	0

	Strongly Agree	Agree Somewhat	Undecided	Disagree Somewhat	Strongly Disagree
28. I'm willing to keep trying, even when a task is tedious.	4	3	2	1	0
29. I share my possessions with others willingly.	4	3	2	1	0
30. I have prayed with a person in distress and the person was comforted.	4	3	2	1	0
31. I feel comfortable when people drop in unexpectedly.	4	3	2	1	0
32. I pray for others often and for significant periods of time.	4	3	2	1	0
33. Through study of the Bible and other resources I have learned many helpful insights.	4	3	2	1	0
34. Visiting people in retirement homes and/or hospitals gives me great satisfaction.	4	3	2	1	0
35. It is easy for me to make friends in a new community.	4	3	2	1	0
36. It is exciting to provide spiritual leadership for a congregation.	4	3	2	1	0
37. I believe God will lead us through situations others feel is impossible.	4	3	2	1	0
38. I like to share scripture to comfort or encourage others.	4	3	2	1	0
39. I enjoy doing routine tasks for the glory of God.	4	3	2	1	0
40. I enjoy teaching individuals and/or classes.	4	3	2	1	0
41. I derive spiritual meaning from music, art, or nature.	4	3	2	1	0
42. I enjoy helping others find solutions to life's difficult problems.	4	3	2	1	0
43. I like to organize people to enable more effective ministry.	4	3	2	1	0
44. I do not fear leading people in spiritual matters.	4	3	2	1	0
45. I don't mind helping people who are sick or disabled.	4	3	2	1	0
46. I can sense the difference between truth and error.	4	3	2	1	0
47. I am drawn to share my faith in God with others.	4	3	2	1	0
48. I like encouraging inactive church members to become involved again.	4	3	2	1	0
49. I am sure of God's loving presence, even when things are seemingly going wrong.	4	3	2	1	0

	Strongly Agree	Agree Somewhat	Undecided	Disagree Somewhat	Strongly Disagree
50. I appreciate being able to give my skills and energy in a critical situation.	4	3	2	1	0
51. I feel called to be a part of the healing ministry of the church.	4	3	2	1	0
52. People feel very comfortable in my home.	4	3	2	1	0
53. God consistently answers my prayers in tangible ways.	4	3	2	1	0
54. I have learned much about God from scripture, books, and observing life.	4	3	2	1	0
55. I gain joy from comforting people in difficult situations.	4	3	2	1	0
56. I am able to relate to and communicate with people of different locations or cultures.	4	3	2	1	0
57. I like to assist people with their spiritual problems.	4	3	2	1	0
58. I believe that when I am doing God's will, God can and does work through me.	4	3	2	1	0
59. I enjoy relating God's Word to the issues of the day and sharing this with others.	4	3	2	1	0
60. When there is something to be done I am glad to help but I don't want to be in charge.	4	3	2	1	0
61. People learn readily when I teach them.	4	3	2	1	0
62. I can communicate well with people who are limited by a physical or mental disability.	4	3	2	1	0
63. I can help people find the truths they seek.	4	3	2	1	0
64. I like the challenge of making important decisions.	4	3	2	1	0
65. I enjoy sharing God's word with others.	4	3	2	1	0
66. One of my ministries is helping other people bear their burdens.	4	3	2	1	0
67. I have helped people discover God's will in their lives.	4	3	2	1	0
68. I have shared spiritual experiences with a neighbor who doesn't attend church.	4	3	2	1	0
69. People who are feeling perplexed often come to me for encouragement and comfort.	4	3	2	1	0

	Strongly Agree	Agree Somewhat	Undecided	Disagree Somewhat	Strongly Disagree
70. When everyone is discouraged – including myself – I still trust God.	4	3	2	1	0
71. If I can't give much money to support God's work I give generously of my time.	4	3	2	1	0
72. I feel at peace when I am with a person who is sick or injured.	4	3	2	1	0
73. I like to have missionaries or church leaders visit my home.	4	3	2	1	0
74. I pray for others, recognizing their effectiveness and well being depends on God.	4	3	2	1	0
75. Knowledge of the Bible and of church teachings helps me to solve problems in daily life.	4	3	2	1	0
76. People think I am a kind, compassionate person.	4	3	2	1	0
77. The thought of beginning a new church in a new community is exciting to me.	4	3	2	1	0
78. People bring their troubles and concerns to me because they feel I care.	4	3	2	1	0
79. People think of me as one who believes that with God everything is possible.	4	3	2	1	0
80. It is important for me to speak out against wrong in the world.	4	3	2	1	0
81. I find more satisfaction in doing a job myself than in finding someone else to do it.	4	3	2	1	0
82. One of my joys comes in training people to be more effective in living out their faith.	4	3	2	1	0
83. I can make sense of specialized information (like computers, blueprints, accounting, etc).	4	3	2	1	0
84. I feel that I have insight in selecting workable alternatives in difficult sitations.	4	3	2	1	0
85. When I am in a disorganized group I tend to be the first one to get things organized.	4	3	2	1	0
86. I enjoy training workers in the congregation.	4	3	2	1	0
87. If a family is facing a serious crisis, I enjoy the opportunity to help them.	4	3	2	1	0

	Strongly Agree	Agree Somewhat	Undecided	Disagree Somewhat	Strongly Disagree
88. I look beneath the surface and discover richer meanings.	4	3	2	1	0
89. I feel a concern for the people in my area who have not been attracted by the church.	4	3	2	1	0
90. I am like a cheerleader, cheering others on when they are doing something well.	4	3	2	1	0
91. Even when it seems that my prayers go unanswered, I keep praying.	4	3	2	1	0
92. I give of my time, talents, and resources because I know God will meet my needs.	4	3	2	1	0
93. I feel strongly that my prayers for a sick person are important.	4	3	2	1	0
94. I have opened my home to someone in need.	4	3	2	1	0
95. I find myself praying even while I am doing other things.	4	3	2	1	0
96. I find it an enjoyable challenge to read and study a difficult book of the Bible.	4	3	2	1	0
97. I find great satisfaction in visiting people who are confined to their homes.	4	3	2	1	0
98. I desire to talk to people of other ethnic backgrounds about our respective understandings of God.	4	3	2	1	0
99. I enjoy a close relationship with people in a one-on-one situation.	4	3	2	1	0
100. I will take on a difficult task because God will see me through.	4	3	2	1	0
101. I feel called to stand up for what is right even if it irritates others.	4	3	2	1	0
102. I like to do things without attracting much attention.	4	3	2	1	0
103. It is easy to organize materials for teaching a Bible class.	4	3	2	1	0
104. I have a knack for foreign languages, American Sign Language or Braille.	4	3	2	1	0
105. I have confidence in dealing with problems.	4	3	2	1	0

Spiritual gifts profile sheet (Part one)

Name _____ Date _____

Directions: Put your score for each question into the following table, then compute the sum of each row. This provides the score for each spiritual gift. The score will range from 0 to 20 for each gift.

1 ___	22 ___	43 ___	64 ___	85 ___	= ___	Administration
2 ___	23 ___	44 ___	65 ___	86 ___	= ___	Apostle
3 ___	24 ___	45 ___	66 ___	87 ___	= ___	Caregiving
4 ___	25 ___	46 ___	67 ___	88 ___	= ___	Discernment
5 ___	26 ___	47 ___	68 ___	89 ___	= ___	Evangelist
6 ___	27 ___	48 ___	69 ___	90 ___	= ___	Exhortation
7 ___	28 ___	49 ___	70 ___	91 ___	= ___	Faith
8 ___	29 ___	50 ___	71 ___	92 ___	= ___	Giving
9 ___	30 ___	51 ___	72 ___	93 ___	= ___	Healing
10 ___	31 ___	52 ___	73 ___	94 ___	= ___	Hospitality
11 ___	32 ___	53 ___	74 ___	95 ___	= ___	Intercession
12 ___	33 ___	54 ___	75 ___	96 ___	= ___	Knowledge
13 ___	34 ___	55 ___	76 ___	97 ___	= ___	Mercy
14 ___	35 ___	56 ___	77 ___	98 ___	= ___	Missionary
15 ___	36 ___	57 ___	78 ___	99 ___	= ___	Pastor
16 ___	37 ___	58 ___	79 ___	100 ___	= ___	(Deeds of) Power
17 ___	38 ___	59 ___	80 ___	101 ___	= ___	Prophet
18 ___	39 ___	60 ___	81 ___	102 ___	= ___	Serving
19 ___	40 ___	61 ___	82 ___	103 ___	= ___	Teaching
20 ___	41 ___	62 ___	83 ___	104 ___	= ___	Tongues
21 ___	42 ___	63 ___	84 ___	105 ___	= ___	Wisdom

Spiritual gifts profile sheet (Part two)

In the spaces below, list your gifts in descending order of score. Use the List of Spiritual Gifts for further study.

Interpreting the numbers

16 - 20 – You are either doing this or you should be. God has plans for you in this area.

11 - 15 – You could easily do this if you desire. God can use you in this area.

6 - 10 – You would have to work hard to do this gracefully. You will want to ask God about this area.

0 - 5 – You most likely would not enjoy doing this. It is likely God has plans for you outside this area.

Score	Gift
———	———————————————————
———	———————————————————
———	———————————————————
———	———————————————————
———	———————————————————
———	———————————————————
———	———————————————————
———	———————————————————
———	———————————————————
———	———————————————————
———	———————————————————
———	———————————————————
———	———————————————————
———	———————————————————
———	———————————————————
———	———————————————————
———	———————————————————
———	———————————————————

List of spiritual gifts

The Spiritual Gifts Test helped you determine which spiritual gifts you have. The questions assessed your gifts in 21 areas. Below are descriptions of each of those 21 areas. The descriptions include scripture references as well as a suggested listing of some church roles. You'll notice the church roles all end with a blank. This is so you can fill in your own ideas of where you can use your gifts within your congregation.

Administration – The Holy Spirit enables some to motivate, direct, and inspire God's people in such a way that they voluntarily and harmoniously work together to do the church's work effectively. To exercise the gift of administration is to assume oversight for the proper execution of an organization or program (being in charge of people or things). This gift involves being able to put things together, tie up the loose ends and get things done. You will set a pattern for others to follow by direction, instruction, guidance, and encouragement of example. Adeptness at financials, planning, organizing, delegating responsibilities and problem solving can be indicators of the gift of administration.

References: Exodus 18:13-16, Judges 3:10, and Hebrews 13:7

Ministries: Committee chairperson, building committee chairperson or member, treasurer, conduct annual audit, youth leader, organize outreach events, attend meetings and conferences, convention delegate or alternate, organize receptions or family nights, coordinate scheduling of volunteers, _____.

Apostle – The Holy Spirit enables some to lead, inspire, and develop the church of God by proclamation and the teaching of truth. To exercise the gift of apostleship is to perceive and accept God's call to lead others in their spirituality. You acknowledge God's grace and authority in the life of the church. This gift involves being able to lead others wisely and compassionately as well as training others in spiritual matters. Apostleship includes a combination of wisdom, discernment, leadership, and teaching.

References: Matthew 4:18-22 and Acts 14:21-23

Ministries: Sunday school teacher, neighborhood canvasser, participant in justice causes, _____.

Caregiver — The Holy Spirit empowers some to willingly bear the burdens of others and help them in such a way that they can do their tasks more effectively. To exercise the gift of caregiving or helping is to give assistance or relief from distress where it is needed. This gift involves a willingness to help others even when the jobs may be messy. The jobs may also involve getting into close proximity to people who are sick or distressed.

References: Matthew 25:34-40 and Acts 6:2-4

Ministries: Greeter, usher, youth leader, concerns of the elderly, concerns of the disabled, volunteer work, assisting in church programs, working in the church kitchen or office, fundraising, helping others carry out their own ministries, —————————————————————.

Discernment — The Holy Spirit enables some to discover the will of God. To exercise the gift of discernment is to distinguish between truth and error. It is to identify whether something is of God. This gift involves wisdom and prayerfulness.

References: Proverbs 17:24, Hosea 14:8-9, and Acts 5:3-6

Ministries: Counselor, pastoral caregiver, hospice volunteer, spiritual director, serving on a committee to employ and deal with church workers, —————————————————————.

Evangelist — The Holy Spirit enables some to share the Gospel with others in such a way that they come to know God. To exercise the gift of evangelism is to share one's faith within and beyond your congregation. This gift involves an unabashed willingness to "be religious."

References: Acts 8:26-40 and 2 Timothy 4:5

Ministries: Evangelism committee, membership/newcomers committee, inquirers' class teacher, greeter, usher, prison ministry, campus ministry, participation in renewal events, —————————————————————.

Exhortation — The Holy Spirit empowers some to stand beside other people who are in need and bring comfort, counsel, and encouragement so they feel helped. To exercise the gift of exhortation is to call forth the best from others. This gift involves helping others to be more dedicated in living out their faith, bolstering them up when they are discouraged or downhearted and challenging them to see the goals to which God calls them.

References: Acts 11:23-24 and Acts 14:21-22

Ministries: Committee chairperson, pastoral caregiver, justice projects, working with young people, ministering to church staff members, preaching, working with the elderly or disabled, writing letters of encouragement, prison ministry, —————————————————————.

Faith – The Holy Spirit provides some with extraordinary confidence in God's promises, power, and presence so they can take heroic stands for the future of God's work in the church. This gift involves a healthy prayer life, sensitivity to the will of God, and a firm trust that God will come through, even when there is no concrete evidence.

Reference: Hebrews 11

Ministries: Tithing, stewardship committee, project supporter, social ministries committee, prayer chain, Bible study participant, building committee member, _____.

Giving – The Holy Spirit enables some of us to offer our energies, abilities, and material resources for the work of the church with exceptional willingness, cheerfulness, and generosity. To exercise the gift of giving, one operates out of a spirit of selflessness, requiring no recognition or reward for one's giving. This gift involves offering one's time, energy, talent, skills, material possessions, and money.

References: 2 Corinthians 8:1-5 and Matthew 6:1-4

Ministries: Tithing, stewardship committee, project supporter, flowers for services, Christmas gifts for less fortunate, participating in church programs and projects, _____.

Healing – The Holy Spirit leads some to share in restoring the sick. To exercise the gift of healing is to pray not necessarily for a cure but for God's help for the sufferer. It is to pray that something of good may come out of the distress. This gift involves a healthy prayer life, confidence in God's power to provide courage in suffering and wellness of spirit regardless of the condition of the body or mind.

References: 2 Kings 5:1-3, 9-14, Luke 9:1-2, and James 5:13-16

Ministries: Pastoral caregiver, prayer chain member, participate in healing ministry of the church, visit the sick, visit in hospitals, intercessory prayer with or for the sick, _____.

Hospitality – The Holy Spirit enables some to open their homes willingly and offer lodging, food, and fellowship cheerfully to other people. A concern for the comfort of others may be a manifestation of the gift of hospitality. This gift involves making people feel at ease, enjoying being in the presence of strangers, and being willing to open one's home as ministry.

References: Genesis 18:1-8 and Hebrews 13:1-2

Ministries: Small group host, help with church suppers and events, Sunday coffee host, greeter, usher, membership/newcomers committee, entertaining church guests, _____.

Intercession – The Holy Spirit enables some to pray intensely and for extended periods of time with a great positive effect for the building of the kingdom. The gift of intercession is praying for others, a vital and important ministry. Evidences of the gift of intercession would include having the mindset to be instantly in prayer for a person or situation, having confidence that God acts in response to our prayers, being patient and persistent in prayer even when change is not evident and having a continuing sense of responsibility to pray for people and situations.

References: 1 Thessalonians 3:10-13 and 1 Timothy 2:1-2

Ministries: Prayer chain member, private prayer, prayer groups, prayer vigils, praying with others, _____.

Knowledge – The Holy Spirit enables some to understand in an exceptional way the great truths of God's Word and to make them relevant to specific situations in the church and in daily life. To exercise the gift of knowledge one must enjoy learning. This has probably been instilled from childhood and has carried through into adulthood. This gift involves the knowledge of facts and relationships, of scripture and the tradition of the church, and of the lives and works of church fathers and mothers. It also includes knowledge of the ways of sharing these learnings gracefully.

References: Hosea 6:6 and Ephesians 3:14-19

Ministries: Preacher, Sunday school teacher, Bible study leader, marriage mentor, attend seminars and conferences, _____.

Mercy – The Holy Spirit enables some to feel exceptional empathy and compassion for those who are weak or suffering such that they devote large amounts of time and energy to alleviate these conditions. To exercise the gift of mercy is to relate to others in kindness and compassion. This gift involves continual readiness to forgive those who have erred, comfort the bereaved, help those who face a crisis, minister to the sick, become a peacemaker, or offer assistance to those in need.

References: Micah: 6:8 and Luke 10:30-37

Ministries: Pastoral caregiver, hospice volunteer, prison ministry, AIDS ministry, deaf ministry, poverty ministry, race relations, nursery care, visit the sick or shut-ins, call on lapsed members, participate in programs concentrating on social needs, care for the disadvantaged, comfort the bereaved, _____ .

Missionary – The Holy Spirit enables some to minister in a second culture or second community. To exercise the gift of missions is not to impose one's beliefs on another, but to faithfully and mutually share what one has learned about God. This gift involves a willingness to be and share with people of different heritage, customs, economic background, and experience. It also includes a willingness to listen more than speak, and awareness that God loves all people.

References: Mark 16:15-20 and 1 Corinthians 9:19-23

Ministries: Community service volunteer, Meals on Wheels volunteer, Hispanic ministry, soup kitchen, sponsor a refugee family, prison ministry, migrant worker ministry, foreign missions, _____ .

Pastor – The Holy Spirit enables some to assume responsibility for the spiritual welfare of a group within the church. The gift of pastoring is not necessarily the ordained ministry. This gift includes leading worship, pastoral counseling, and leadership in church programs.

Reference: 1 Peter 5:1-11

Ministries: Pastoral caregiver, spiritual director, worship committee member, pastor, _____ .

Deeds of Power — The Holy Spirit empowers some to accomplish much toward achieving God's will in our church and community. (In some versions of scripture this gift is called the working of miracles.) This gift involves a firm and faithful relationship with God, courage in the face of adversity, and a willingness to call on the power of God.

References: Micah 3:8, John 14:11-14, Acts 1:8, and 2 Timothy 1:5-7

Ministries: Prison ministry, poverty ministry, hunger ministry, race relations, participating in programs concentrating on social needs, caring for the disadvantaged, comforting the bereaved, _____ .

Prophet — The Holy Spirit empowers some to interpret and apply God's revelation in a given situation. This gift involves a keen sense of the dignity of all people, a sense of call, a sense of timing, and knowledge of scripture and the workings of the church.

References: 1 Corinthians 14:1-5, 1 Corinthians 14:30-33, and 1 Corinthians 14:37-40

Ministries: Preacher, counselor, Bible study leader or participant, convention delegate, _____ .

Serving — The Holy Spirit enables some to willingly share the burdens of others and help them in such a way that they can do their tasks more effectively. To exercise the gift of serving is to identify closely with the needs and problems of others. Not necessarily providing answers or solutions, but being willing to work with them, no matter how small or large the task may be. This gift involves a willingness to pitch in and do whatever is needed, no matter how detailed or tedious the task.

References: Galatians 6:1-2 and Philippians 2:3-8

Ministries: Committee member, Meals on Wheels volunteer, office volunteer, landscape volunteer, lawn mower, snow removal, nursery worker, Habitat for Humanity, soup kitchen, Red Cross blood drive, social ministries committee, food bank, poverty ministry, migrants ministry, choir, music, repairs around the church, cleaning the church, painting, _____ .

Teacher – The Holy Spirit enables some to communicate so that others can learn. To exercise the gift of teaching one effectively imparts information or proclaims precepts of truth vocally, visually, or by example.

References: Isaiah 28:9-10 and Hebrews 5:12-14

Ministries: Sunday school teacher, youth leader, tutor, train other volunteers, day care volunteer, work with young people, social ministries involving teaching or training others, _____.

Tongues – The Holy Spirit enables some to communicate or to understand in forms of communication beyond the ordinary. To exercise the gift of tongues is to communicate in or understand a foreign language or anything (such as ASL, Braille, art, and music) other than our own native language.

References: Psalm 104:2-35 and Acts 2:5-11

Ministries: Hispanic ministry; ministry for the deaf or blind; poverty ministry; sharing meditations on art, music, or nature; expressing one's faith through art or music, _____.

Wisdom – The Holy Spirit endows some with an understanding of God's will and work as it relates to the living of life. To exercise the gift of wisdom is to help others discover the wisdom they have within themselves. This gift involves knowledge of God and scripture, discernment of God's will, and skill in analyzing the problems and dilemmas of life.

References: Ecclesiastes 9:13-18 and James 3:13-17

Ministries: Counselor, spiritual director, convention delegate, youth leader, pastoral caregiver, hospice volunteer, _____.

Consider again

After reviewing the descriptions, especially for your top three to five gifts, consider these questions again:

- Do I agree with the results? Why or why not?

- Am I using my strongest gifts? What do I need to do differently?

- Are there gifts I would like to make stronger? How would I do that?

- What does this exercise lead me to do now?

Sources

1   The Spiritual Gifts Test and accompanying material were compiled from a variety of sources found on the Web. Most of these did not have formal titles or authors listed.

2   Johannes Eckhart, German Dominican author.

Bringing stewardship to life

*If you enjoyed "*Talent Show: Your Faith in Full Color,*" you will want to consider the other books in MMA's Living Stewardship study series, including* **"Time Warped: First Century Time Stewardship for 21ˢᵗ Century Living."**

In "Time Warped," Steve Ganger, MMA's director of stewardship education, provides:

- Twelve flexible, interactive lessons on how to "do less" yet create a more fufilling relationship with God.

- Practical Scriptural applications that ground each lesson in God's Word.

- Personal time chart and planning documents that help you take immediate action.

- Helpful group discussion questions that encourage deep, personal reflection.

- Encouragement and ideas that will motivate you to make lasting life changes now!

MMA's *Living Stewardship* study series examines holistic stewardship from the inside out in the areas of time, talent, money, health, and relationships. Each book deals with one area of stewardship – but in a holistic way.

You will think about stewardship in new ways as you work through these titles – and more books are in the planning stages now! Visit MMA-online (www.mma-online.org) to learn more about holistic stewardship.

Living Stewardship books and other educational resources, are available in the MMA Bookstore (www.bookstore.mma-online.org) or call (800) 348-7468, Ext. 269.

Bringing stewardship to life

If you enjoyed "Talent Show: Your Faith in Full Color," *you will want to consider the other books in MMA's Living Stewardship study series, including* **"Money Mania: Mastering the Allure of Excess."**

In "Money Mania," Mark L. Vincent, a consultant with Design for Ministry, provides:

- Twelve flexible, interactive lessons that take readers beyond budgeting to visit various intersections in life where money plays a significant role.

- Practical Scriptural applications that ground each lesson in God's Word.

- Pointers to help you be earnest about your faith and organize your finances in ways that honor God.

- Helpful group discussion questions that encourage deep, personal reflection.

- Encouragement and ideas that will motivate you to make lasting life changes now!

MMA's *Living Stewardship* study series examines holistic stewardship from the inside out in the areas of time, talent, money, health, and relationships. Each book deals with one area of stewardship – but in a holistic way.

You will think about stewardship in new ways as you work through these titles – and more books are in the planning stages now! Visit MMA-online (www.mma-online.org) to learn more about holistic stewardship.

Living Stewardship books and other educational resources, are available in the MMA Bookstore (www.bookstore.mma-online.org) or call (800) 348-7468, Ext. 269.